Onna Rashiku
(Like a Woman)

Onna Rashiku
(Like a Woman)

The Diary of a
Language Learner in Japan

Karen Ogulnick

State University of New York Press

Published by
State University of New York Press, Albany

For information, address State University of New York Press,
State University Plaza, Albany, N.Y. 12246

Production by M. R. Mulholland
Marketing by Fran Keneston

Library of Congress Cataloging-in-Publication Data

Ogulnick, Karen, 1960–
    Onna rashiku (Like a woman) : the diary of a language learner in
Japan / Karen Ogulnick.
        p.   cm.
    Includes bibliographical references and indexes.
    ISBN 0-7914-3893-7 (hardcover : alk. paper). — ISBN 0-7914-3894-5
(pbk. : alk. paper)
    1. Japanese language—Study and teaching—English. 2. Language
and culture—Japan. 3. Ogulnick, Karen, 1960–   . I. Title.
PL519.0338 1998
495.8′007—dc21   97-45140
                                                                CIP

10 9 8 7 6 5 4 3 2 1

To my friends in Japan,
domo arigato gozaimashita.

Contents

Acknowledgments

To begin with, I thank especially Keio, Akemi, Satoko, and Mayumi (whose real names I cannot mention due to confidentiality) for their patience and generosity in teaching me Japanese. Without them, this book could not exist.

I was first formally introduced to Women's Studies when I began my doctoral program at New York University. The feminist process that was used in many of my classes opened up a tremendous amount in me. I became compelled to analyze further my experiences as a woman. Women's Studies gave me a set of tools with which I could begin to grasp the dynamics of gender and other types of identity politics, and to locate various inequities in social interactions.

I am indebted to my professors and fellow doctoral students in the English Education and Women's Studies programs for contributing to my empowerment as a writer, reader, thinker, and speaker. To all the people with whom I've shared so many important learning experiences, thank you.

In particular, I'd like to mention a few people who over the years have helped me enormously with their personal, intellectual, and technical support, profound insight, and confidence in my work: my doctoral committee at New York University, Gordon Pradl and Berenice Fisher; my dissertation support group, Gail Verdi and Barbara Leopold; and Robert Roth, who redefines the word friendship with all the time, energy, heart, and soul he put into reading, commenting on, and listening to me talk about my manuscript.

For their love and encouragement, I thank the Ogulnicks, Kriegsteins, and Mottas, Stephanie Hart,

Sharon Shelton-Colangelo, Jay Shmulewitz, Daniel Shure, Victor Wheeler; and a special thank you to Cheryl Williams for calling that evening in November 1992 to ask me if I would like to teach in Japan.

I am deeply grateful to Priscilla Ross and Jennie Doling of The State University of New York Press for all their efforts in getting this book published, and to Lynn Becker Haber, Keith Gilyard, George Jochnowitz, and Ned Jackson, for their thorough, critical, and timely readings of my manuscript. And for the beautiful calligraphy on the cover of this book, I thank Nori Jung.

To the superb colleagues, staff, and excellent students I have the privilege of working with at Long Island University/C. W. Post campus, thank you for supporting my work and providing me with infinite opportunities to continue to learn as a teacher.

1

Introduction: Traveling

There is a woman who looks familiar, yet very different. I am watching her on a videotape. She has my face, hair, and body, but her actions and speech are someone else's. She is sitting *seiza* [on her knees]. Her movements are confined and controlled. She is speaking a foreign language. When she laughs, she raises her hand and delicately covers her mouth. Although she looks different from the Japanese women in the video, she seems to fit into the environment.

The video was made in 1987, at the end of my second year in Japan. Traveling was not new to me the first time I went to Japan in 1985. I feel I have always been a traveler, moving in and out of different spaces. Let me go back to the beginning.

I am now 8 years old and with my grandfather, my first traveling companion. I clutch his hand as we cross the street and enter into Bronx Park. The city streets are far behind as I climb freely up and down the rocks along the winding river path that leads into the zoo. We always stop along the way to sit on a certain bench, and grandpa points to a spot where he tells me it said "Lou loves Mary" a long time ago.

I try to imagine my grandmother sitting on that bench with my grandfather. Grandma doesn't come with us to the zoo; she is too busy—cooking, cleaning, washing, shopping. Sometimes grandma travels back to her childhood in the stories she tells of growing up in a small town near Odessa, in a house with flowers in a garden. She is uprooted from this home when she is 12, when her father is killed and the rest of her family is persecuted for being Jews.

Grandpa becomes very playful when we are away from home. He tells me stories about the "friends" we meet at the zoo, or, as he usually refers to the apes and gorillas, "relatives—on the *other* side of the family." Grandpa has another beer before we say good-bye to our caged friends and return to the other side of the zoo gates.

I remember wanting to go away, somewhere far, ever since I was a small child. Maybe it is because my mother went away when I was very young. She had a nervous breakdown and committed herself to a mental hospital not long after she aborted her third pregnancy. I can still hear my father's voice yelling, "Murderer!" After spending a year in Creedmore in the mid-1960s, my mother came back home. But her mental health never returned. I don't remember her very much after she came back. One day I clearly remember. I had just started third grade. I came home from school and found everything boxed up—and my father all ready to go. My mother wasn't home and I didn't want to leave her. But I didn't say this. I was too frightened that he would leave me too and take my sister with him. I was 7 years old and afraid to speak.

I never questioned my mother's mental illness. I was told she was "sick" and I believed it, even though she didn't really seem sick when I talked to her or visited her in the various mental hospitals in which she lived. But what else could it be? She had been diagnosed by a doctor, after all.

Now I am in Mrs. Specter's fifth-grade class. I write a horror story about people being tortured with red-hot irons and cut up into tiny pieces. I show it to Mrs. Specter and eagerly await her glowing response. "You don't use the word 'caution,'" she reprimands as she hands the paper back to me. Maybe she sensed some problems and didn't want to deal with anything except for my vocabulary deficiency. This was one of the last pieces I remember writing for school. I must have been using plenty of caution.

I am 19 and traveling around the world. As I cross international borders, I feel free and powerful. I move around open and trusting of people. I begin to write again. I write about my week-long climb up the Himalayas with two guys who treat me as a climber and not a "girl." I write about the time I almost drown in the middle of the Sunda Straits when our small banana boat sinks, and then, after finally being rescued, taken to (and then left on!) a small deserted island. I write about the people I meet—the brief, intense encounters, the families who let me stay in their homes. I imagine these stories will someday turn into a wonderful book. However, the journal that makes it all around the world gets lost shortly after I return home, when I pass it into the hands of a family member.

I am now 29 and traveling around the world again. I don't feel as free and powerful as I had 10 years before. One night in India, I am brutally and violently assaulted by two men. I close down completely. I can't breathe the air anymore, so I dive into the sea and learn how to breathe underwater. Deeply submerged as I am, everything is quiet. I concentrate only on the sounds of my breath. Inhale. Exhale. The heavy tank on my back becomes lighter. The sharks no longer scare me. After several months underwater, I resurface slowly, and, for the first time since I lost my journal, I begin to write once again.

Making my personal life public brings up many fears—fear of revealing my secrets, fear of rejection, fear of attention, fear of getting hurt. The risks I'm taking and lines I'm crossing by writing openly about my experiences as a woman in the world seem even more dangerous than some of the travel experiences I've had. But

I believe these risks are necessary in order to evolve, to live life more fully, to uncover thoughts and feelings that for so long have been hidden and smothered, and to hear my voice amid the din of other people's voices.

2

A Redhead in Takefu

Even before the plane touched down in Japan, I began to experience the different language. What seemed as if it took 10 seconds to say in English turned into a 3-minute translation in Japanese. I thought about how in Japanese there is a more ceremonious and polite way of saying and doing things. As I took in my surroundings in Narita airport I was aware of how, unlike JFK, everything appeared clean, safe, orderly; I felt myself moving at a slower pace. A process was beginning.

In 1985 I was employed by the Japanese Ministry of Education to teach English in Japanese public junior and senior high schools. At first I was not particularly interested in going to Japan, but after 3 years of teaching in the New York City public schools, the opportunity to teach in a different environment seemed very appealing.

Three of the English teachers who were assigned to supervise me during my stay met me at the train station when I arrived for the first time in Takefu, a small city in the rural, farming district of Fukui. Due to it being the rainy season in Japan, it was a typically wet June day. My supervising teachers helped me settle into my new apartment and stayed with me until late that evening. The next morning, Sunday, Ina-*sensei* [teacher] arrived bright and early to show me around my new neighborhood—which looked like a maze of winding, twisted, unnamed streets. There was not a sign of English anywhere. I was convinced that I would get lost immediately if I ever tried to venture out of my apartment on my own, and then I would never be able to ask anyone how to get back.

On introducing me to each neighbor, Ina-*sensei* bowed and humbly requested, *"Dozo yoroshiku onegai shimasu"* [Please think kindly of her]. My landlord was an elderly woman who did not speak a word of English, but she and my next-door neighbor came by frequently to bring me food, "talk," and keep me company. Between the three supervising teachers, my landlord, and neighbor, I felt I could hardly turn around without someone being there, eager to assist me.

Although I appreciated their kindness, there was a distinct feeling of loss involved. It was a persistent tug and pull between the independence and autonomy I had taken pride in developing from my upbringing, and the new set of expectations I perceived the Japanese had that I acquire what I considered the less virtuous qualities of being young, weak, and dependent. Suddenly, I wasn't sure if I was the same person who had left home at 17, financed her own college education, and traveled around the world alone at 19, or, an infantalized 24-year-old woman who needed to be helped and taken care of.

The dreariness of the month-long rainy season was occasionally brightened by moments of recognition that I was in a unique and exciting situation. As the only American English teacher in the area, I had become, for better or worse, an instant celebrity. Heads constantly turned as people passed me from behind, wondering who that "crazy" Japanese woman was with her hair permed and dyed red. (This I knew from what people told me they had thought when they first saw me.) On glimpsing my face, people seemed to be really surprised, for I was the first "real" foreigner they had ever seen.

My experiences made me assume a particular status, but this status changed from one situation to another. In some circumstances, I was treated as if I were helpless, such as when I attempted to travel to the next town by myself, whereas in other situations I would be expected to do things that I had never thought I could do—such as to present a speech to an audience of over a thousand people. If only they had known what a painfully shy person I was, I probably would not have been able to perform many of the acts they expected of me. But I couldn't be shy. The Japanese, I was informed, are shy, whereas Americans are outgoing.

I made no attempt to learn Japanese during my first three months because I thought it would be impossible. I had no time to study, and, besides, almost everyone I met wanted to practice English with me. I rationalized my decision not even to try to learn Japanese by telling myself that, one, it was too difficult and, two, the Japanese Ministry of Education was not paying me a generous salary to speak Japanese. I also resisted learning Japanese since I did not consider myself a "good language learner," after several earlier, unsuccessful attempts to learn a foreign language. However, after about three months of daily exposure to Japanese, I had an experience that led me to begin to notice that, despite my resistance, Japanese was somehow finding a way to slip into my consciousness.

The event occurred while I was riding on a streetcar one day on my way to work. An elderly woman, about my grandmother's age, entered at one of the stops and, despite the fact that the train was empty, sat down right next to me. She began to talk to me in animated Japanese. I cut her short with the one phrase I had managed to memorize to prevent incidents like these from occurring, *"Zenzen wakarimasen"* [I can't understand a word of what you are saying]. This comment did not seem to discourage her, however, from continuing to talk to me. I gave up trying to tell her that I truly couldn't understand Japanese and just smiled and watched her as she spoke. When we arrived at her stop, I waved her off, saying the one other word that comprised the rest of my entire active Japanese vocabulary, *"Sayonara."* Once alone with my thoughts, it occurred to me that something significant had happened: I had understood some of what she had said, something about the weather, and she hadn't spoken a word of English. I distinctly remember this incident because that was the moment I discovered to my amazement that it might actually be possible for me to learn Japanese.

My experiences as an American woman speaking Japanese revealed that, from 1985–1987, speaking to foreigners was not something with which most people in rural regions of Japan had much experience. When I could hardly utter a word, people were quick with praise: *"Nihongo ga o-jyouzu desu ne"* [You speak Japanese very well]; but when I began to make an earnest attempt to string words together, I often encountered blank stares. The incongruity of my white face and Japanese speech seemed to prevent people from psychologically registering that I was speaking Japanese. It was also difficult getting people to adjust their speech to my level. Perhaps due to their inexperience with speaking Japanese to foreigners (especially English teachers), when people spoke to me it seemed to be in one of two extremes: either in baby Japanese or "the real thing."

Even as my fluency developed and began to surpass the level of English that was spoken to me, people often did not acknowledge my attempts to communicate with them in Japanese. On noticing how American men were responded to in Japanese, I began to consider that gender might be a factor that contributed to my not being taken seriously as a Japanese speaker. In spite of these obstacles, constant daily exposure to the language and my increased motivation to learn enabled me to develop basic social fluency by the end of my first year in Japan.

Along with the verbal language, I acquired new body language and increased awareness of levels of politeness and formality required in certain social settings. Through observations of Japanese people speaking, as well as their reactions to the way I spoke, I realized that in Japanese there are different words, tones, and parts of speech for women and men. With a head full of red curly hair, I was unmistakably non-Japanese. While my foreign status granted me some flexibility in terms of how I was expected to speak to whom, I also felt that my identity kept me frozen in a certain place, from where I could never really be taken seriously as a Japanese speaker, perhaps even as a woman. Nevertheless, my desire to fit into the culture as much as possible not only produced in me softer, more polite ways of speaking, but also created changes in my movements, actions, feelings, and my perception of myself as a woman. It also made me straighten my hair.

Through the traveling my job required, I met many women with whom I only briefly became acquainted. The intimate details women shared with me of their private lives reminded me of the way people sometimes tell fellow travelers their life stories. While being invited in this way into people's lives made me feel like an "insider" in Japanese society, telling me these stories, often in English, may have been a way for Japanese women to connect their private lives to the outside world. The women who befriended me, and even those I hardly knew, told me tales of forced arranged marriages and their subjugated positions in their "husband's home" that made me feel glad to be an American woman: I felt I was freer than these Japanese women I had met. Despite the image of Japan as a supermodern society that had been promoted by the U.S. press, I thought I had traveled back to a time when women were controlled and restricted to activities and roles revolving around the household. Conversely, I felt comfort in the relationships I was building with Japanese women and, along with my disdain for the traditional roles they played, I admired what I perceived as their inner strength and their clear sense of self, which I felt was lacking within myself.

Looking back, I can see that I was observing "them" as if their situation had no relevance to mine. In my reimmersion into Japanese culture several years later, and even more so in 1993, the experience was more like looking into a mirror—not one that reflected back my exact image, but one that revealed, even where there were differences, much about the condition of being a woman in my own culture. This time by being there, and being aware of how I was learning Japanese, I was also learning the many subtle and not-so-subtle ways I had been taught to speak "like a woman" in my native language and culture.

3

An American Jew in Hiroshima

In the mid-1980s Japan was on the cover of almost every major news magazine, all of which had been promoting extremely positive images of everything Japanese from cars to computers to raw fish. There seemed to be an enormous effort to extol Japan as a model for the United States. Much of the attention was triggered by Ezra Vogel's best-seller *Japan as Number One,* published in 1979, in which he focused on Japan's booming economy and corporate success. The Japanese system that ostensibly took care of its people from cradle to grave became idealized by the American public. We were fed reports on Japan's "model" educational system, which produced diligent students, high IQ scores, less than 1 percent illiteracy, and the Japanese corporation, which guarantees employees lifelong employment and, in turn, fosters a devotion that comes second to none, including devotion to self and family.

The Japan I saw contrasted sharply with the ultramodern, affluent, homogeneous image that had been promoted by the U.S. media. I taught English to a wide variety of people. Students in the "top" high schools most closely resembled the U.S. media's stereotyped image of the diligent Japanese student. Most of the students I taught, however, were on commercial and technical tracks. I also taught in the "low" schools, which were created for students who broke the school rules. To be sure, the most interesting English classes took place in these schools, since we weren't confined to the standard curriculum. I was also surprised to see, not far from where I was living, a residential area that was comprised of old, run-down shacks. Even more surprising was what a Japanese friend told me when I asked, "Who lives there?" "Can't say the word," the friend insisted. "It's taboo in Japanese." Eventually, I also obliterated their existence from my mind. It wasn't until years later, through reading some literature on *Burakumin* (literally, people of a subvillage, or "ghetto"), that I discovered who these "taboo" people probably were: native Japanese who are believed to be "dirty" and "crazy" due to intermarriage genes. Like India's "untouchables," in Japan these people are the "unmentionables."

Due to the tremendous rise in the number of English-speaking foreigners in Japan, the English language became the primary symbol of "internationalism." Internationalism indeed became a very popular fashion in the 1980s, which seemed rather peculiar, since Koreans, Chinese, Filipinos, Pakistanis, Iranians, Brazilians, and many other internationals had been living and working (often illegally) in Japan long before then.

Internationalism in Japan in some ways parallels multiculturalism in the U.S.—although the starting points for each of these movements differ. When Japan became part of a global economy in the eighties, many businessmen found themselves having to work in an international community. Thus, internationalism, on the one hand, was primarily concerned with learning how to deal with people in the outside world. Multiculturalism in the United States, on the other hand, is a matter of finally developing respect for the diversity that has always existed within America—accepting that "outsiders" can become "insiders." While both of these movements represent an expanded view of the world, they each have their limitations: Japan permits that "foreigners" can be accepted as long as they register their "alien" status with the government; similarly, many people in the United States, even those who give lip service to "diversity," can be, at their very best, tolerant of people of different races and cultures—so long as the "others" are striving to be English-speaking, apple-pie eating "Americans."

The different attitudes people in the United States and Japan have toward foreigners are also reflected in the two countries' different treatment of foreign languages—whereas the United States assimilates foreign words into English, Japan represents words of foreign origin as "loaned" or "borrowed." There is even a separate dictionary for Japanese "loanwords." These very terms, when referring to language, reveal an ideological bias. After all, who are the "borrowers" and who are the "lenders"? And how are these "loans" paid back?

Looking historically at the relationship between Japan and the United States may provide some insight into the answer to this question. After World War II, when the United States rewrote Japan's constitution, English loanwords reflecting Western lifestyles invaded Japanese vocabularies, influencing Japanese society and ways of thinking. New ideological currents, such as "internationalism," "liberalism," and "democracy," flowed from political levels into Japanese mainstream life. However, even though the words may have created a new awareness, they didn't necessarily lead to changes in behavior or attitudes. For example, although the Frank Sinatra tune, "My Way," remains a favorite in the Karaoke bars, and has become a Japanized-English expression (*meiwei*) used to indicate a personal preference, the concept of "individualism" in Japan remains overshadowed by more prominant concepts such as cooperation, community, and group harmony (*wa*).

Just as English words were thought to reflect more liberal and democratic ways of thinking in postwar Japan, the current linguistic manipulation of English words in Japanese today (Haarman, 1989) may reflect Japan's increased confidence gained from a strengthened economy. At least that was the message conveyed in the title of Ishihara Shintaro and Morita Akio's popular book published in 1989, *The Japan That Can Say No.* Or perhaps the message is that Japan is still struggling in its quest for autonomy from the country that has played such a dominant role in its twentieth-century history.

Living in Japan, I noticed that the United States left permanent marks not only in the Japanese language but on the very face of its culture. In Tokyo I saw Western ideals of beauty etched in stone on the many sculptures that can be found in tiny pockets of the city. Salient images of beauty promoted by Hollywood have been responsible for countless cases of cosmetic surgery among Japanese models and actresses, who have had their eyes enlarged, noses heightened, and skin whitened. Greater aesthetic appreciation for Japanese features may correspond with the increased freedom young people have to express themselves these days.

In 1987, I noticed that the Japanese media focused a lot on America's social problems. There were several highly publicized cases of Americans living in Japan at that time. Two American English teachers had committed suicide and one had been arrested on drug charges. The subject of much attention, these incidents cast grave doubt on whether Americans had the emotional integrity and responsibility necessary to teach Japanese students. Even former Prime Minister Nakasone contributed to the anti-U.S. sentiment by announcing publicly that Americans were lazy and inefficient—and that this situation was basically due to blacks. But, many Japanese were quick to explain, this was not a racist comment. For, "We [Japanese] are a homogenous country and so we have no experience with racism" (Buruma, 1986). Nevertheless, the comment, as well as the U.S. Reagan administration's *pro forma* condemnation of Japan's arrogance, hurt and angered a lot of

American people, many of whom felt that what Japan had articulated overtly very much reflected the United States' more covert antiminority policies.

At the same time, a peculiar kind of ambivalence toward Japan was developing in the United States. Although conservatives in the United States continued to glorify Japan's disciplined, authoritarian (and possibly "genetically pure") system that got people to produce, an anti-Japanese mood was being openly expressed by various strands of the public. American labor unions were smashing Japanese automobiles. Popular American movies made fun of Japanese culture. Japanese were labeled "copycats" by U.S. electronic companies.

The following event, which a friend described to me, seems to capture the climate of senseless bigotry taking place in the United States in the late 1980s, at a time when Japanese-U.S. relations were particularly hot:

> One sweltering summer day in New York City a Jewish man waited in his Japanese girlfriend's apartment while an air conditioner was to be delivered. A black man arrived with the air conditioner. As he placed the heavy box down, the boyfriend noticed the man's sweat-soaked Harley Davidson tee shirt, which said, "I'd rather my sister be in a whorehouse than ride a Jap bike." The girlfriend happened to return right at this critical moment. The boyfriend retreated into another room while the other two encountered each other.

Meanwhile, anti-Semitic voices in Japan were becoming more outspoken. Books were published in Japan about an "international Jewish conspiracy," consisting of wealthy bankers, businessmen, and landowners who were planning to take over the world. Such propaganda was widely circulated in the popular press and still appears in popular Japanese comic books.

I reentered Japan for the third time in 1993, at a time when the country was experiencing a period of significant economic decline. Aronowitz and DiFazio (1994) describe the situation as follows:

> In stark contrast to the 80's hype of the invincibility of the Japanese, especially its effective corporatism, the early 1990s witnessed severe changes in the Japanese economic outlook. For the first time since the early postwar years, many of the largest corporations such as Mitsubishi laid off thousands of workers, cut production, and began to transfer work to less developed countries. (p. 6)

Most immediately visible to me was how the economic decline effected the students and teachers at the university in which I worked. Promises had been made that could no longer be kept. American teachers complained bitterly about having to pay Japanese taxes for the first time (even though we didn't have to pay U.S. taxes). Students were suddenly told that they had to go to the United States in order to graduate. And even then, there was no guarantee that they would find a job on returning to Japan, since graduates from prominent Japanese universities were not being hired by the major companies in which they had been expecting to work.

In an even more personal sense, living in Hiroshima in this period of major economic and social upheaval made me more aware of my historical and national relationship to Japan. Whenever I went into Hiroshima City, once the site of unimaginable horror, now "The City of Peace," I would see Hiroshima Dome, or what was left of it. This served as a striking reminder of what was always there, rarely mentioned directly, but often referred to obliquely—the bombings of Hiroshima and Nagasaki. My identification with the country that dropped these atomic bombs on Japan, and Japan's alliance with Germany during World War II, made the connection I perceived to the Japanese a precarious one. Many questions remain unanswered, much goes unspoken, but somewhere in the background of my relationships with friends in Japan, these legacies of the past are still there.

4

The Pillow Book of Learner Karen

January 24, 1993, Hiroshima

One of the first things I noticed on arriving in Japan was how clumsy and awkward I felt, especially whenever I went to pay for something. It took me a long time to get my money out and to count it, since I had forgotten what Japanese money looks like. People seemed outwardly patient, but I could sense some irritation with waiting. I also felt watched quite a lot, a very different feeling from being in New York, where I usually feel so anonymous. The first thing I saw when I got off the bus in Hiroshima was the outside of Sogo department store. Young Japanese women wearing violet Hilary Clinton hats and perfectly matching violet suits stood absolutely motionless like mannequins at the doors, ready to open them for customers, I presumed. Looking at the people walking around the streets of Hiroshima, I noticed a marked distinction between old and young women. Young women looked girlish—and the old very old. The young women were dressed fashionably and seemed bright and cheerful, whereas many elderly women looked sad and miserable. Their clothes were gray, plain, and drab, but most striking of all was the lifeless expressions on their faces. I wonder if this is a result of living through the trauma of the atomic bomb.

I've begun to speak Japanese a little. I was glad to find all was not forgotten after not having spoken it for 2½ years. It took so long to learn, I really don't want to lose it. I spoke to the bank teller a little, telling her that I would like to exchange money. She responded to me in English. This might have been because I spoke very hesitantly; in fact, I felt somewhat embarrassed speaking Japanese. I think it will improve soon, though. Walking around, and looking at the youth-oriented shop displays decorated with balloons, bright colors, dolls, and cutesy, childish-looking things, made me feel older. It was a strange feeling—I caught a glimpse of myself as I passed a mirror and I even thought I looked older.

The bus from Hiroshima to Chiyoda, the town where I am living, took an hour and a half. I traveled with a fellow American colleague. She doesn't speak Japanese and remarked about how "dumb" that makes her feel. I can recall a very similar feeling when I first lived in Japan and wasn't able to speak or read the language. As she put it, "It's like being a baby, but worse." This time those particular feelings aren't coming up for me, but I am experiencing similar feelings of insecurity that seem to be evoking unpleasant thoughts about my childhood lately. This morning a traumatic event flashed through my mind. It was an incident that occurred when I was about 6 years old. I was surprised it came up because this particular one is not a scene that is often replayed in my memory. It was of my father picking up my doll carriage and throwing it at my mother, missing her, but crashing my doll carriage against the wall. I was very attached to my doll at that time, and was completely devastated that its carriage was broken. I remember running into my bedroom and crying. This morning I also recalled the time (it could have been the day after the doll-carriage fight) when we had a TV repairman, a telephone repairman, and a man to

repair the refrigerator all in our apartment at the
same time. One of them said, "You must have had
a wild party here last night." It was wild all right,
but no party. These memories could be related to
the feeling I am experiencing here—of not being
able to speak. My father's violence certainly
silenced me—I never knew when I might be suddenly struck—sometimes for crying, sometimes for
saying a "bad" word.

I also recalled the "tit" incident, which I hadn't
thought of for a long time. I was only about 6 at the
time. I was sitting in my father's car, looking at a
picture of a pinup girl on an air freshener hanging
from his rearview mirror. Thinking she was beautiful—and that my father must have thought so too
and that's why he had her picture hanging in his
car—I announced that when I grew up I was going
to "let my tits hang out just like she does." Suddenly, he slapped me on my face. "Don't ever say
that word," he said, as he continued to slap me
repeatedly. What is bringing back this memory? Is
being in Japan bringing up feelings of fear? Am I
afraid of saying something wrong?

Jan. 26

I tried to stay up and study some Japanese
last night, but I couldn't keep my eyes open after
8:00. Jet lag. I'm also fighting a cold. The large bal-
cony windows next to my bed feel like the walls of
a freezer when I touch them. Any attempt to heat
the apartment is counteracted by the draft that is
pulled in where the curtains fall short of the floor.
Despite the extremely poor insulation, the apartment is nice. It's small, but cute and cozy, and,
best of all, fully equipped with everything I need.
The college generously provided all the basic fur-
nishings plus a color TV, microwave oven, washing
machine, and dryer, and today as I looked in the

closets and cupboards I discovered some other goodies: a blender, wok, glasses, dishes, a vacuum, bathroom soaps, towels, and even some cans of food. These help make me feel more comfortable— and not having to buy this stuff here also helps my at-the-moment not-so-great economic situation in this land of the rising yen.

This morning I awoke to a blanket of white. The view of the mountains from my third-floor apartment is gorgeous. I had to walk across the snowy soccer field in my sneakers since I forgot to pack any kind of shoes for snow. How could I have forgotten with all the shoveling I did the last time I lived in Japan? Orientation consisted of filling out more forms—immigration, school policies, bills, et cetera. Then I had to go into town for photos and to be fingerprinted for an alien registration card, which I am required by law to carry around with me at all times. A poster hanging on the wall at the town hall caught my eye. It was of a young man carrying a baby. I asked someone to translate what was written in Japanese underneath it. It said: "Even though men don't have breasts with which to feed their babies, they still have a lot to give." That was the first sign of change I have noticed since I've been back in Japan.

Jan. 27

Woke up at 5 a.m. Still sick. Called a friend in New York to wish her a happy birthday. Hearing a familiar voice made me cry. I miss my friends. But there are some nice people around here. I've been spending some time with two female colleagues, Nancy and June, since we are in the same "orientation" group. June invited me to dinner tonight, but I decided to stay in and keep my germs to myself. She brought over some oranges, which was very nice. June is a tiny Korean woman, about 50, full of energy. She speaks Japanese and English fluently since she grew up when Korea was occupied by the Japanese and it was compulsory that all subjects be taught in Japanese. She got her PhD at the University of Chicago. She is the school counselor. I enjoyed her company for a little while. We briefly talked about our feelings being here—we both seemed to feel pretty positive so far, although we joked about the obsession with paperwork. It felt comforting not to feel entirely alone here.

Jan. 28

Today we had a "faculty outing" to a nearby "city"—Miyoshi, about an hour's ride by van. On seeing a road sign to Matsue on the way back, we talked about the writings of Lafcardio Hearn, who lived in Matsue. One faculty member talked about Edwin Reishauer, saying how wonderful it was that he persuaded the U.S. to spare Kyoto, the cultural capital, when they were bombing Japan, so that the national treasures housed in the many museums and temples wouldn't be destroyed. I felt a chill go up my spine: Was it more "wonderful" to spare culture than people?

Jan. 29

This morning the weather was nice and sunny, which made it hard to stay indoors, despite all the work I had to do to prepare for my classes. Ann, one of the American college staff members who lives in my building, called me in the morning to let me know she would be in all day and available to take me to "Thanks" (the supermarket!) if I needed anything. That was nice, but I felt like exploring on my own, so I cycled into town and tried to get my bearings. I think I know where "everything" is now, which didn't take long, since there isn't much here. There's "Thanks," the bus station, 7-Eleven, the

community center, and some other small shops.
(After shopping in Thanks I understood why it is
called that—with the prices they charge for food,
they should say "Thanks"!) I stopped in the community center to ask about classes. I did it mostly to
practice my Japanese since I already had a class
schedule. An old man and woman were there. I
could hardly understand the old man's Japanese—
he must have been speaking Hiroshima-*ben*
[dialect]. I couldn't understand a word he said. The
old man called the woman to come and talk to me.
She was very cheerful and seemed eager to explain
things—and I could understand her Japanese. I
found myself apologizing for bothering her. She
refused the apologies but told me that it would probably be better if I came back when the classes are
running. Then I went into 7-Eleven, just to see what
kinds of junk food they had in there. Naturally I ran
into another faculty member, who was doing the
same thing. We oooed and aaahed over Haagen-
Dazs, Oreo cookies, and frozen burritos. Then, I rode
down the main street checking out the small family-
run shops. I stopped in one little grocery store. A
man who looked like he was in his thirties was the
only one working there. I was the only customer and
he stayed nearby, "in case [I] had any questions,"
which indeed I had, mostly for practicing Japanese.
I carefully scrutinized all the "exotic"-looking items
that were crammed into this tiny shop. I explained
to him that I had only recently arrived and still did-
n't know many things about the food here. He smiled
and seemed willing to help. I asked about the
spaghetti sauce, whether it had meat in it. He told
me they all do. And about the curries, which were
hot and which were sweet, about the assorted pick-
les and what the contents were of various condi-
ments in jars. The pickled garlic looked the most
intriguing, so I bought it and some other interesting

items. He asked me how long the flight took from
America to Japan. I told him that it took fourteen
hours from New York. He shook his head in disbelief. Before leaving I asked for directions back to the
campus (which I really needed) and he patiently
explained them to me, and even offered to draw me
a map, but I told him that wasn't necessary. As I left
he said, *"Kiyo sukete"* [take care].

Jan. 30

Last night Nancy, June, and I went to the public baths at the base of the campus together. The
baths seem to be the most popular evening activity,
besides watching CNN, of course. It was Nancy and
June's first experience in a Japanese bath, and
interesting to see their reactions to having to bathe
nude publicly. I don't think Nancy was quite expecting that—but she got the idea when she saw me
take off all my clothes. We washed with the hand
showers outside the baths before soaking. There are
three different baths—one big hot one, a smaller
jacuzzi, and an electric one, which I will avoid since
there was a sign that said "radon" over it. Soaking
in the hot tubs with these women was an ice
breaker, so to speak, but I am finding it increasingly
difficult to maintain my privacy here. When you live
so close to people you work with, it just doesn't
seem appealing to bathe with them at the end of the
day—although there is a sense of comfort in not
being all alone. I've noticed that some of the non-
Japanese faculty members who have been here
longer seem to be withdrawn and rather reclusive. I
bet this existence does that to you—when there is
no privacy you have to build your own walls.

Jan. 31

Every time I come back to Japan, I have to ask
myself, "Why?" Do I get amnesia and forget what a

hardship it is to live here? Everything requires so
much more energy: shopping, cooking, eating,
speaking, bathing—even getting out of bed, since
there is no central heating here. It seems all people
do here is work, work, work. I'm also feeling claus-
trophobic. It seems that everywhere I go I run into
other faculty members—the supermarket, baths,
even in Hiroshima city. There is no escaping them.
And since we live and work together, I feel I have to
be so nice and polite all the time. I don't think I'm
really cut out for small-town living. I'm also beginning to get frustrated that I don't seem to have
enough contact with Japanese people—and not
enough chances to speak the language. The Japanese staff at the college don't seem to interact much
with the American faculty members. They seem so
busy all the time—and not very approachable.
There are two women about my age who look as
though they stepped off the pages of a fashion magazine. I feel, more than I ever had in New York, self-
conscious of my gender-neutral clothing. Stan, the
male music teacher, and I dress almost identically,
in jeans and sweaters, but this attire is fine for
him. However, I might have to go out and buy more
formal clothes for teaching. At least it's easy to find
my size here.

February 2

This morning I woke up with a huge, swollen,
red eye. What seemed like a sty yesterday had gotten a lot worse and more painful, so I decided to
cancel my 9:00 class. I called the office at about
8:30 to let them know. Then at about 8:40, my
doorbell rang and it was Chihoko, the Japanese
secretary to the dean. I wasn't expecting her and
felt kind of embarrassed to let her into my apartment, which was a total disaster area. She didn't
seem to pay much attention to it, although I know

she did. She went straight to my phone to call the office to tell them that she would be taking me to the doctor. I said that it wasn't necessary for her to go to the trouble of taking me to the doctor. I said (in Japanese) that I could go to the pharmacy and buy some medicine. (I wonder if this offended her.) She said she was thankful to be able to leave the office. We were both quiet in the car so I began some small talk—in English, but her answers to my questions were short and she didn't initiate any more conversation, so I just sat back and enjoyed the pretty mountain scenery, still covered with the early-morning thick mask of fog. The countryside in this area is mountainous and densely wooded with pines and bamboos. Most of the homes I saw in the area are large, traditional, Japanese farmhouses situated on the edges of rice fields. There were some small houses, but they seemed to be part of larger estates. There were lots of little children in red and yellow caps (red is for elementary school students and yellow for the preschoolers). They looked like little chicks walking in lines to school. The boys were wearing short shorts—supposedly to make them "tough" in winter. The girls had longer skirts on and jackets.

Chihoko drove a bit far out of town, following someone else's rather vague directions that she should keep driving until she reached a "narrow road." Sure enough, we reached a narrow road and there was an eye clinic. The waiting area was already full by 9:00, mostly with elderly people. I was asked to sit for a little while, but I certainly didn't have to wait my turn. Even though there were many others before me, I was only about the third person to be called. The nurses spoke to me in Japanese, which I understood at first. When the doctor spoke to me it was in English (his was pretty good), but he mostly spoke to Chihoko in Japanese, most of which I couldn't understand. Suddenly, while he was examining my eye he pulled it roughly, which caused me to gasp loudly in pain. He said in Japanese to Chihoko (which she translated later): "American doctors are gentle with their patients because they are afraid of getting sued, but I will do it the Japanese way." When the nurses tried to speak to me in Japanese after that, I couldn't understand them, nor could I speak to them in Japanese. Chihoko translated for me while I was in the pharmacy purchasing the medicine the doctor prescribed. Chihoko was more talkative on the way back and I also felt more relaxed and started to speak in Japanese.

A significant part of my reimmersion in Japanese was exploring my new environment and entering into a different social context—different both from America and from the Japan I had previously known. In contrast to my first visit to Japan, when I was highly dependent on my supervising teachers to show me around my neighborhood and introduce me to people, from the moment I arrived this time I had some ability to function independently in the language. Although my first attempts to speak in this setting, as recorded in my diary, convey tentativeness and embarrassment at not being able to speak well, that I actively sought out opportunities to speak Japanese suggests that I experienced a feeling of comfort in being able to do so, even with my limited capacity. In the particular situations I was in, people in relation to me spoke in a way that felt encouraging. In some sense, I experienced an instant affirmation and gratification from being able to speak Japanese—I often did not have to say very much in order to be understood. Perhaps my wanting to go off alone, where English wouldn't be spoken, was at least partly driven by a quest for the possibility to claim both independence and autonomy from my native language, and to achieve an identity as a language learner.

The recurring theme in my diary of wanting to stand apart from, yet connect with others reflects a conflict I felt between immersing myself in Japanese or American culture. My decision to get away from the security of speaking English with another American and explore my new environment on my own reveals a preference to be in Japanese language and culture. The feeling of "claustrophobia" I expressed in my diary above, of not being able to "escape" from the people with whom I lived and worked, also suggests that being with English speakers may have felt constricting, somehow keeping me from being able to absorb the stimuli of my new environment and learn the language.

But, before letting me go off in another direction, my childhood memories kept calling me back, beckoning me to reconcile myself with what I have known. My memories were right there behind me, whispering in my ear, reminding me of times I have not felt safe venturing out on my own in unfamiliar territory. Although the anxiety I experienced as an adult language-learner was not as raw as the nightmares brought on by trauma in my childhood, the flashbacks that were triggered were intense.

My father's violence in response to my exploration of my sexuality taught me that there are parts of me that had to be hidden, that were taboo even to mention. This was a lesson on how to invalidate my reality, to move away from my body, and quite possibly, to turn myself into a version of a person without breasts. I was taught not to speak about my body, and to replace the pleasure of self-discovery with guilt and shame.

A significant part of learning language involves learning muteness, learning to submit. It therefore does not seem to be a coincidence that some of my most painful memories of being molded by my social context were evoked when I was silenced in Japanese. Although the doctor articulated his intention to treat me as he did other Japanese patients, by calling attention to this treatment, he in fact highlighted my difference. Thus, contrary to what could have been his conscious intention, I felt I was being spoken to and treated a certain way precisely because I was presumed to be different from Japanese people. I was the other, one of "them."

The women—Chihoko and the nurses—spoke to me in a way that enabled me to speak, understand, and be somewhat in control of a situation in which I already had little control, while the doctor—and only man in the office—took this capacity away. By not letting me understand or talk back, he made a frightening experience even more painful. I experienced that as a way of his using language to keep me controlled. I wonder if this was "the Japanese way," to which he referred. Although my anxiety was undoubtedly heightened due to the linguistic and cultural barrier, the feeling of not being in control of my body was not completely foreign to me. In fact, I had experienced that "way" before.

Suddenly being aware of the role of power in my personal relationships and learning was frightening: it was as if I were a participant observer of my own passivity and restraint. While the process was not as visible to me in my first language and culture, there are similar assumptions about care in asymmetrical power relationships, such as those between doctors and patients, parents and children, teachers and students, men and women, which are based on the idea that the person of lower status must submit to the control of the person of higher status. Although I gasped loudly in pain, I conformed to the cultural expectation of showing respect by submitting to the doctor. Not only did I behave solicitously in order to deflect negative attention from myself, I may have done so in order to establish some solidarity with Chihoko, who seemed to be friendlier on the way back from the clinic. "The nail that sticks out," a well-known Japanese proverb echoes, "gets hammered down."

Learning a language involves learning rules, restrictions, what I can and cannot say. Likewise, as I move in and out of my diary, I am conscious of crossing a border between private and public. There are certain contexts in which it feels safer to be open than in others. I am often intuitively aware of where these lines are drawn. Traveling in and out of these spaces, I am constantly shifting voices, each of which is shaped by different external constraints.

When learning a language in another culture, one simultaneously takes in and is taken in by the social context, even one that feels alienating. Japan and I had undergone some profound changes since my previous visits. It was very important for me to absorb these changes right from the beginning, as these early observations formed a crucial first stage of developing a sense of where I was in relation to the context in which I was attempting to communicate. Feeling the mood of my environment was vital in my ability to move within the rhythms of Japanese language and culture. This allowed me to relate to people in a shifting culture, rather than remain static in my previous impressions of Japan and its people.

Signs of change in gender roles for young Japanese men and women seemed to reflect a change in attitudes toward marriage and child care. Like Chihoko, most unmarried Japanese women were concerned about marriage and lived at home with their parents; however, unlike the situation I observed 8 years earlier, there did not seem to be the same degree of urgency for women to get married before their 26th birthday, before becoming what I myself had been warned by older Japanese women against becoming upon turning 25, a piece of "old Christmas cake."

To be sure, what I perceived as a clear demarcation between young and old women in Japan made me, as a 32-year-old single woman, hear my "biological clock" tick more loudly than I ever had before. As I described in my diary above, while forming my first impressions, an image I saw reflected back to me in a mirror looked older than the one I remembered in the United States. An important factor affecting the different perceptions Japanese and American women have of age and aging are the different points at which women are expected to go through significant life stages. These stages seem to be greatly affected by what Berenice Fisher (1991) calls "family/community time frames" (p. 94). Since more single Japanese women live in tightly knit family/communities than single American women, there is less room to negotiate these time frames; however, with increases in economic independence and longevity, a shift is occurring among Japanese women—many more remain single or marry and have children later in life. Although in the United States I was aware of being an age in which women were marrying and having children, in the family-oriented community in which I lived in Japan, I became more conscious that I was approaching or indeed at an age that many Japanese considered *osoi* [too late].

Men's lack of involvement in domestic affairs feeds into women's increased resistance to marriage. The poster I noticed at the town office of the young man carrying an infant may reflect a new movement for males to play a more nurturing role, a role that has been traditionally reserved exclusively for women. Or, could it have been another form of sexist propaganda? Was the subliminal message that child care isn't a burden for women, since, after all, husbands help care for their children? But do men really want to help women with child care? Or do they just want to usurp one of the few domains of power women have—as caregivers?

These early diary entries convey the power of the environment in shaping my perceptions of how I was supposed to act, move, listen, and speak. Right from the beginning I became self-conscious about my age, clothing, physical appearance, how I spoke, how people spoke to me. I was being socialized through implicit understandings of my place, understandings that there were penalties involved for not acting properly, and approval granted when I capitulated. Flashbacks to childhood experiences brought me back to times when I was controlled, punished, and sexually suppressed. Although I perceived gender-specific codes of appearance to be more prominent in Japan, thinking back to my own cultural socialization process, I recall the gender-polarizing ways I was taught how to speak, act, and look like a girl. I can still hear echoes of men's voices commenting on my clothes, hair, body—each one in conflict over how I should look—more modest, sexier, thinner, fatter, older, younger. Each one had an image around which I tried to mold myself. The two societies and languages may have been different, but the message that I received, implicitly and explicitly, was basically the same: that women's bodies, language, and thoughts are controlled by men.

5

Keio and Me

I remember how fascinated I was by the Japanese art of gift wrapping, *tsutsumu*, the first time I went to Japan, especially on seeing how even my everyday purchases would be carefully wrapped in beautiful Japanese paper. As a foreigner in Japan, I could only observe from the outside. My desire to "fit into" and be accepted by the society in which I lived and worked, and my motivation to become more proficient in Japanese, made me very attentive to the ways people acted, moved, spoke. These impulsions also made me a willing participant in my own process of compartmentalization: a new public, outer self encased the inner. I became wrapped up in pretty packaging.

Just as I have felt boxed in by gendered categories, my initial judgment of Keio, a Japanese man with whom I traded English lessons for Japanese, shows in my diary below that I was engaging in the same process—confining him to a particular "type" based on his appearance. It seems that I had a great deal of confidence in my ability to do this—to make predetermined judgments of people whom I did not know. Indeed, it felt like an achievement, something I had developed through increased self-understanding and experiences in interpersonal relationships. However, the culturally determined lens through which I could only see Keio as awkward and uptight obscured me from seeing things beneath the surface, such as his sensitivity and vulnerability. Although I was not consciously aware of my attitude at the time, this undoubtedly played into and created an obstacle in our interactions and, consequently, in my language-learning experiences.

Jan. 26

Last night I met Keio for the first time when a bunch of us went out to Clementine's, a "country-western" bar in Hiroshima City. There was an American singer from Nashville—Pat Dakota. We ordered various "Tex-Mex" specialties, such as pizza with corn and seafood on it, "om-rice" (an omelette filled with rice), and some other dishes. We also ordered lots of pitchers of beer. The place was not large, and it was packed. Except for the singer and the three other non-Japanese at our table, everyone else seemed to be Japanese. Keio, a staff member at the college, was the only Japanese with us. When he first arrived and sat down right next to me I thought he was just another clone *"sarariman"* [businessman]. He looked kind of nerdy in his typical office uniform: blue polyester suit, white starched shirt, and red tie—and large dark-framed glasses. (I was dressed casually in jeans.) Keio introduced himself to me rather formally—gave me his meishi [business card] and spoke to me in not-so-good English. Robert (a male American staff member and friend of Keio's) told him that I could speak Japanese. I said it wasn't very good, but we ended up talking most of the night in Japanese. At first I felt somewhat inhibited talking to him in Japanese, but I seemed to relax considerably the more my beer glass was filled.

Toward the end of the evening Robert, an American staff member at the university, suggested that we (Keio and I) become language-exchange partners. I reacted enthusiastically and I think Keio also thought it would be a good idea. I think he will be a good partner since we are about the same level, so we can struggle together.

Before the alcohol began to take effect, the diary entry reveals that I was highly aware of the formality Keio projected in his speech, behavior, and appearance; and, as my somewhat contemptuous and telling characterization of him reveals, I did not view it favorably. At closer look, it seems that what he represented to me made me feel uncomfortable. His formality symbolized the rigidity of the Japanese language and culture, with its emphasis on protocol, politeness, and form. As a man in a business suit, he also symbolized everything male to me: the public world of power and privilege.

Our daily lunchtime conversation usually took place in an empty classroom on the sixth floor of the academic building of the college, the building in which we both worked, I as an English teacher and Keio as an administrator. We sat facing one another in small, hard classroom chairs with two desks in between us. The presence of a small tape recorder on the desk reminded us that our conversations were being recorded. Although I felt more relaxed speaking outside of the college environment, the empty classroom in which Keio and I met offered privacy and isolation that seemed to make me feel less self-conscious speaking Japanese than I did in the more public faculty lounge.

While this was the least restrictive place within the college building, it still felt confining to me, which may have been why I often suggested that we also practice outside of the college—at my apartment (which was convenient since I lived on campus), at a coffee shop in town, or while having dinner together in a restaurant. A closer look at the different ways I perceived our interactions in different environments reveals an assumption that, because we occupied the same space at the same time, we were in the same physical "worlds." Our shifting roles and verbal behaviors in the different environments, however, suggest that we had contrasting perspectives of "inside" and "outside."

In Japan there are certain rituals people perform

38   *Onna Rashiku (Like a Woman)*

that mark the passage from outside to inside. Even though I lived in a "Western-style" apartment in Japan, there was a feature that remained distinctly Japanese: the *genkan* [entranceway]. Very often, Japanese guests will open the front door themselves and enter into the *genkan,* announcing their arrival, but they do not usually walk past the *genkan* area into the rest of the house before hearing their host's formal polite expression, "*Irrashaimassei*" [welcome], inviting them in. Before entering a Japanese home, people always remove their outside shoes and replace them with a pair of indoor shoes, or slippers, provided by their host. The custom of bringing something from the outside when visiting someone's home also symbolizes the inside-outside transition. The gifts are usually food or flowers, but they vary widely. I recall my surprise once, for example, when I opened an elaborately packaged pine-scented box to find inside a large hand-picked aromatic mushroom, dirt and all. (I later learned that this was a very luxurious item.)

That Keio did not perform any of these rituals suggests that, whereas my apartment represented an *uchi* [home] context to me, enabling me to be more relaxed, spontaneous, and unreserved, for Keio, the very same environment represented *soto* [outside], requiring him to maintain formality, restraint, and reserve (Rosenberger, 1994). I had not realized that being in my own apartment seemed to make me feel freer to indulge myself in ways that being outside in the larger environment did not. My expectation that Keio also would feel relaxed when we were in my apartment was based on an assumption that a person can actually feel "at home" when she or he is in fact in someone else's home. In English, people are often told to make themselves at home when they are in other people's homes. In Japanese, however, a parallel expression does not exist. On the contrary, neither the host nor the guest are ever really expected to be "relaxed" in such a context.

I preferred to practice Japanese with Keio in my apartment because being there made me feel less constrained about how I could express myself. Although at the time I was not very focused on the sexual implications of our meeting there, in retrospect, I don't know what, if anything, it meant to Keio to have been invited into my apartment. The one time I recall feeling that there may have possibly been some sexual attraction on Keio's part to me occurred in my apartment, when, at one point in the conversation, he touched my leg briefly. I felt mildly uncomfortable about it because I did not want us to have a sexual relationship; it's very possible that he didn't either, but being touched in my apartment, for me at least, seemed to, for this one moment, shift my perception of our relationship. I also recall feeling somewhat self-conscious once when an American colleague saw Keio leaving my apartment at about 11 a.m., and gave us one of those smiles that suggested that she thought he had spent the night.

That I perceived Keio as uptight suggests that he may have experienced different environments differently than I did. The places that seemed less formal and unconstraining to me were for Keio steps away from Japanese culture, which removed him from a place of power, and might be why he appeared to me to be "uptight" in situations in which I felt more "relaxed." Even though I felt more comfortable in my own apartment, with Keio there, teaching me Japanese, it was clear that I was the *gaijin*, outsider, an American in Japan speaking Japanese.

Since the university was owned and operated by a Japanese businessman, for whom Keio worked, our relationship reflected the hierarchical structure of the Japanese employers in relation to the American employees at the university. Further, because I was employed at the university only temporarily and Keio was a permanent staff member, it is also possible that he felt a greater sense of belonging than I did. The sentiment of loyalty and dedication to one's company is captured in the Japanese phrase often used when referring to one's workplace, *uchi no kaisha* [company family].[1]

Although I felt some sense of belonging to the university, particularly because of my connection with its New York affiliate, the institutional setting of "work" still represented to me a binary opposite to "home." At work, on the one hand, cultural expectations required me to dress, look, speak, and behave in certain ways. Being in my apartment, on the other hand, seemed to give me greater liberty to express myself—verbally and nonverbally—differently than I felt I could in the college environment. The physical environment, the structure of the language and our relationship were all intertwined. When the setting felt abstract and distancing to me, so was my language, and likewise, I perceived our relationship to be more distanced. As the following diary entries suggest, there was a dialectic between my perception of self as an "insider" or "outsider" in relation to Keio and my ability to speak to him in Japanese.

April 1

> Keio just left my apartment. We had an interesting discussion. After an exhausting day, I came home, changed my clothes, and began to feel comfortable. By the time Keio arrived my mood was much better. I was cheerful, talkative, telling anecdotes about all the April Fool's pranks Robert played on me—the computer-virus memo in my box and sending my students to a different room before I got to class. I felt good about my Japanese. Keio wasn't correcting me. I made coffee, sliced up a kiwi, and put some cookies on the table. Keio told me not to bother by using a polite, formal expression, *"Okamai naku"* [Don't go to any trouble]. . . . We began by talking about Robert's party. We talked about the people we had met, etc. I asked

him if he is planning to do any more *hanami*
[cherry blossom celebrations] this spring. He said
he will with his family—his mother, father, and
older sister. This led me to ask him a series of questions about his family. I asked him if his parents
still work. He said that his father works in a school
(his father used to be an elementary school
teacher) and his mother works in a hospital as a
cook. Then I asked if his mother had graduated college. He said that she had graduated from high
school—and began to explain about old high-
schools but he stopped himself in the middle, saying *"Ii desu"* [enough]. I said, *"So desu ka?"* (an
expression of interest), and he continued to explain
about old high-schools—that in those days they
were like college (for women). I asked if his sister
went to college. He said no. I asked, *"Senmon
gakku?"* [specialty school]. *"Iie,* high school *desu."*
[No, high school]. "What kind of work does she do?"
"Government clerk." As he talked about his family
I thought I would like to meet them—especially his
sister, but I didn't want him to feel obligated to do
something he didn't want to do. Besides, his family
might think we are planning to get married or
something. I was also curious about his family's
living arrangements since they seemed unusual
(him living with his sister in an apartment and his
parents living alone in a big house) and what his
parents thought about the idea that he and his sister were remaining single, but I felt this would be
intrusive. Keio changed the subject by asking me
what I wanted to do in the future. I told him, the
same thing I am doing now—teach English. He
suggested that I work for the United Nations. I told
him it was difficult to get a job like that. He said
that I could probably do it. I said that I have more
relevant experience teaching. He asked me if I liked
it. I said that I thought it was interesting some-

times—it depends on the students and the other teachers. I said it is interesting when I am working in a place where teachers share their ideas and I can learn from them. I was masking a complaint, but he didn't show any signs that he picked up on it. Perhaps it was too subtle.

Then, I mentioned the disagreement I had had that day with my coordinator. He frowned but didn't say much. I knew this conversation was probably totally inappropriate, but I didn't care. I didn't know what he was thinking, but the wheels seemed to be turning. I asked him if he ever had any problems with the Americans at our school. He said he has problems not understanding what they are saying or what they are thinking. I asked him if he knew what Japanese people were thinking most of the time, and he said yes. I asked how he knew. He said, "My sense." He said the Japanese place a lot of emphasis on relationships—*wa* [peace and harmony]. I asked him how they do that. He said that in Japanese people use a lot of polite and respectful language. He said that Americans have strong personalities, and they (lock heads) a lot. I agreed and thought about the negative feelings I have been having lately toward some "headstrong" Americans.

When it was his turn to speak English, I asked him if he wanted me to turn on CNN and he said yes. There was a special report on about women. This led to the subject of male and female equality. He said that he thought women in Japan were "stronger" than the men. I mentioned the existence of "OLs" (office ladies) who have to serve tea to the men and do other menial tasks. I said that it seemed that men still have more power in the workplace, and at home women are still the ones who have to do all the housework and cleaning, even though they work outside. He said that there is a clear division of labor in the home, that there is "women's work" and "men's work." I felt myself becoming a little upset by this conversation, but tried to keep my feelings concealed. I mentioned the rising number of single women in Japan, or women marrying later, such as my friend, Asa, who is in her forties and had just gotten married in Tokyo. He said this was unusual.

The following interaction took place 1 week later at the university:

April 8

I'm now listening to a tape of a conversation with Keio. I am talking about my Japanese class, how difficult it is. He interrupts me in the middle of a sentence, using a word I don't understand. So I asked him the word. I still didn't get it, and then I forgot what I was going to say which annoyed me. I practiced from a worksheet that I had gotten in class. He corrects my sentences with complex sentences that I find hard to repeat. He sounds very serious as he corrects me. I am practicing *"toki ni wa"* [when I (do something)]. I am reading very slowly. When I'm reading I don't know what I am actually saying. I pay so much attention to just being able to read the characters, I don't realize that I am actually saying something I can easily understand. As I am practicing, Keio corrects me— but he slightly changes the meaning of what I am saying. For example, I said, "When I drive, I wear a seatbelt." He corrected me by saying, "When I drive, I *must* wear a seatbelt." I repeated him. This session sounds very slow . . . I am bored just listening to the tape. There is no laughter, no real conversation, just me practicing these boring sentence patterns. Finally, in the last 5 or 10 minutes we had some real conversation. Keio used the structures that I had been practicing. Probably because I concentrated more on meaning than structure, I had trouble answering his questions. When I realized that I am supposed to use the structures to answer the questions, I became much more hesitant in answering even very simple questions. I end the session with an exasperated exclamation, *"Nihongo wa muzukashii desu ne?"* [Japanese is very difficult, isn't it?] He didn't say anything. Then, when we switched to English I said, "My grammar is very bad, isn't it?" Keio responded, "No."

One of the things that bothered me about the role Keio assumed as "teacher" was that he played a more active part than I did in my language practice sessions. He often initiated and maintained topics, asked a lot of questions, and filled in gaps when there were impasses. Although I welcomed a corrective and grammar-oriented approach in the beginning (since I was making a lot of mistakes), as I increased my fluency, I began to notice a lack of synchronization between my changing language ability and his static teaching style, or his perception of me as a Japanese learner. The confidence I gained from my increased ability to carry on a conversation was often shaken when the focus shifted to structures and form rather than on meaning.

My experience as a fairly high-functioning speaker and a low-level reader and writer in Japanese gave me a taste of what it is like to be an illiterate adult. The large discrepancy between my oral and literacy skills interferred significantly with my motivation and success in learning how to read or write Japanese. Similar to the feeling I had when I went to Japan for the first time and believed that it would be impossible for me to learn Japanese, I also felt somewhat ambivalent about studying *kanji* [Chinese characters]. However, my resistance to learning *kanji* was not as easily broken, probably because I remained focused on the enormous amount I did not know, rather than the large amount of written language that I was actually absorbing from the environment.

Although Keio's interest in helping me develop literacy skills had a positive effect on my motivation, in the end I actually made very little progress learning to read and write with him. In fact, later entries show considerable resistance to practicing these skills with Keio. My diary strongly suggests that the problem lay in the didactic role Keio played in my practice. Rather than it being a collaborative and interactive process, learning how to read and write with Keio came to mean little more to me beyond the discipline of memorization and repetition.

The growing reluctance and discomfort I felt when writing with Keio was symptomatic of the feelings I had when reading with him. I felt highly incompetent in my ability to read even very simple sentences in a children's book. This was often described in diary entries as "childishness." Keio's attention to *how* I was reading rather than *what* I was reading seemed to contribute greatly to my discomfort. Rather than discussing the content of the book with me, Keio's participation consisted almost exclusively of translating words and correcting pronunciation. A similar process was noted in how I was learning to write in Japanese, as the diary entry below reveals.

April 20

I told him that I wanted to write a card to Asa, so I asked him to help me with that. We spent about fifteen minutes on this. I told him what I wanted to say, but he changed a lot of my sentences by making them more polite. I was a bit dismayed by the fact that he had to correct every sentence. It made me feel that my written Japanese is still very bad. At one point I got annoyed because I noticed that he wasn't only correcting my grammar; he was changing the meaning slightly. For example, he changed "If you are free I would like to meet you in Tokyo" to "If I go to Tokyo I would like to meet you." I told him that the latter wasn't exactly what I wanted to say. He smiled, and then helped me change it to convey my meaning. Then he read it over, and made some more corrections and editing. Asa will be very surprised to receive such a well-written—and polite—note in Japanese from me.

At first glance we see Keio imposing a "standard" form of written Japanese on even a personal note I had written to a friend. However, at a deeper level we see a lot of implicit cultural-knowledge being transmitted in this exchange. For example, Keio's critical scrutiny of my writing reflected a cultural ideology that elevates the status of written over spoken forms of language, teaching me that writing is even more restrictive than speaking in Japanese. Before I even began to learn to write in Japanese, I was already internalizing an editor.

Keio's rewording of my sentence also conveyed the value attached to ambiguity and vagueness in Japanese. Even though there was some miscommunication in the exchange above, I was picking up something about the way Keio was listening—which seemed to be to the subtext rather than the text, which suggests that, along with the verbal language, I was acquiring pragmatic competence. Thus, unlike earlier entries in which I found Keio to be unresponsive to my direct expression of feelings, later entries suggest that I was developing a less direct, more implicit way of expressing myself to Keio, in order to get him to listen and respond to me.

May 6

Keio came over at 8:45 this morning for a two-hour language exchange. As usual he insisted that I go first. So I began by practicing speaking and then I read from my book *Issunboshi*, for almost an hour. It was a bit early for me. I kept yawning. Keio asked me what time I usually get up on my days off. I lied, saying about 8:00 and thought that this must sound very lazy to him. He said that this time was probably too early for me. I said, "Oh no, it's just right" (in Japanese).

I mentioned that I am teaching only one summer course, so I will have a lot of free time from the beginning of June to the end of July. He thought for a moment and then said that he would have more free time too, so he could practice Japanese with me more then.

There was a comfort in being able to communicate things without directly saying them, a feeling of being understood without having to spell everything out. Unlike the relative clarity of direct communication, the ambiguity of indirect communication leaves more room for negotiation. One may choose to notice the silences, or choose not to deal with them. My interaction with Keio below, which took place in a classroom at the university, shows how my difficulty getting through to Keio indirectly forced me to resort to a much more direct, and possibly offensive, way of communicating with him.

May 15

Today's lesson with Keio was extremely frustrating. I was reading out loud from my book, *Issunboshi*, and whenever I came across words that I didn't know, Keio would look them up in a dictionary and give me the translation. I found this annoying, but I didn't know how to convey it. I became quieter. This didn't help so I said it would be helpful if he explained the words to me in simple Japanese, but he either didn't understand this or he just didn't want to do it. It was difficult to continue reading with his constant interruptions. He had his head in the dictionary most of the time I was reading. My reading got slower and my voice lower. He didn't give any verbal reinforcement; he just kept making corrections. I was so tired of the corrections that I stopped indicating when I didn't know a word. I just continued to read, but he kept looking up words in his dictionary again. At one point I stopped reading aloud. Then I said (in Japanese) that I didn't want him to translate words for me, that it would be more helpful if he explained them in Japanese and gave examples. He became silent and glared at me. I asked if we could talk about this part of the book. He told me to finish reading the page, so I did. We finally had some useful conversation about the part I had read in the last five minutes or so.

Although I tried to convey my irritation through silence, my silence did not seem to be noticed, or quite possibly it was noticed, but ignored. Signs of anger, impatience, or frustration seemed to have been interpreted as confrontational, demanding, perhaps even threatening, and therefore to be avoided. In a sense it felt as if I were acquiring two languages: one for saying, and the other for thinking. What I perceived as a lack of responsiveness to my discomfort and frustration gradually caused me to repress these feelings, and to convert them into guilt and shame.

Looking back at myself as a learner in a variety of contexts and with different teachers, I recall how certain individuals were able to bring out my best, to get me to think deeply and expand, while others completely turned me off to a subject. Most of us can recall situations in which learning has been greatly promoted and those in which it has been hindered. More often than not, it is not the subject, but the channel through which we learn that makes the difference between inspiration and boredom, encouragement and despair. When a person extends herself emotionally and intellectually to no avail, she begins to shrink.

There was movement in my relationship with Keio—sometimes close, sometimes distant—which I could not separate from my perception of my language competence. The limitations I perceived in my language ability while talking with Keio often reflected my not knowing *how* to talk to him—the pragmatics of language. Whereas in one context I perceived indirectness to draw us closer together, in another it seemed to be used as a distancing strategy.

It is quite likely that it was not only Keio's grammar corrections and the didactic role he played that created an obstacle between us. Clearly, there was a power struggle going on. When I sought a friendship, he pulled away; when he sought to dominate, I pushed him away. On the one hand, as his behavior suggested and as he confirmed when asked, he perceived our relationship as that of student-teacher (which went both ways). I, on the other hand, saw us as colleagues, even friends (at times), but mostly as two individuals wanting to learn language and setting up situations in which we could help and practice with one another.

The categories Keio and I had available to us in our languages seemed to make it almost impossible for us to ever really speak the same language. Keio's maleness and the role he assumed as *sensei* when teaching me Japanese were dominant images for me; likewise my language, cultural identity, position at the university, and the color of my skin must have represented powerful symbols to Keio. Although at the time I wasn't fully conscious how these symbols came into play in our relationship, one particular incident that occurred toward the end of our 5-month language-exchange, for only a brief period, helped to shift my perception of Keio, and myself in relation to him.

May 27

I showed Keio a list of verbs and said that I wanted to practice them. I said the word in Japanese and he said it in English. I said that I knew the meaning, but I wanted practice using it in conversation. Then he went into long, noninteractive explanations about each word, which wasn't at all helpful. As usual he did a lot more talking than me. I was hardly listening to him, but he didn't seem to notice this. Using one of the words in an example, he brought up yesterday's verdict of not guilty for the man who shot a 16-year-old Japanese boy in Baton Rouge, LA, on Halloween night in 1992. He said that Japanese people don't use guns. This led to a discussion about this case. I expressed my sorrow about the verdict and somehow felt I had to apologize. Then he suggested we practice the words on my vocabulary list. We reviewed about 10 words. Since he corrected every single mistake I made, I felt very conscious of making a lot of mistakes. I spoke very hesitantly and softly. As I listen to the tape, I can hardly hear my voice.

Around the time that the acquittal of Hattori's murderer sent shock waves across Japan, there was increased tension between Keio and me. For a short period, this significantly changed the nature of our interactions. He seemed to respond to my errors even more harshly, yet, strangely, there was something more open about the way he related to me. It began when he referred to the Hattori trial abstractly, using it as an example in a grammar exercise. I hadn't heard the outcome of the case yet, and thus did not at first register the magnitude of what had happened. When such references were repeated over the course of several days and played out in different ways, I began to realize that something suppressed was emerging: it was not my grammar mistakes that angered him. The public rage of the acquittal brought to the surface a deep division between us that had been there all along.

At that time the Hattori trial was an enormous

news story in Japan. It became the topic of intense conversations between people. The tense atmosphere in Japan and the rawness of Keio's emotions stirred up a lot of feelings in me: I felt angry, sad, embarrassed, guilty, and afraid—of returning to a country fraught with violence and racial hatred. I also felt more solicitous toward Keio. It seemed as if for the first time we were looking at the world not from opposite sides, but from a similar place. Mirrored in the anger he seemed to target at me for my white American privilege was the resentment I felt toward him for being a man, for never being able to be hurt in ways that I could be hurt as a woman.

After several weeks there was no more mention of the case. Things between us returned to the way they were before, but traces of this significant event remained with me. I was reminded of the incident many months later, when I was sitting in a movie theater back in New York watching *Rising Sun*, a film sharply criticized by the Japanese for Japan-bashing. At one point I may have laughed along with the audience at the exaggerated and ridiculous stereotypes of Japanese culture; this time I felt I was watching the film from an in-between space— I could both understand why the audience was laughing and I also wondered what was so funny. Just as empathy had shifted my perspective of Keio when I began to see him not only as an "oppressor," empathy for the Japanese people who were being laughed at kept me from joining the audience in making fun of Japanese culture. Although the laughter may have appeared to be innocuous, there was a danger in the racist overtones of the stereotypical images in the movie and pathology of the American public that revealed a sense of anger, hatred, and fear of the Japanese, which was the same anger, hatred, and fear that could allow for what happened in the case of Yoshi Hattori.

6

Akemi and Me

Akemi was one of the people with whom I had the most frequent interactions in Japanese. I met her 2 or 3 hours each week, during which I paid her to tutor me in Japanese. Unlike the situation with Keio, from the beginning Akemi seemed to talk to me very openly about herself, her family, and—a topic that often came up in our conversations—the condition of being a woman in Japanese society. Perhaps because of the 2 years she had spent in the United States, she seemed to have a greater awareness of gender inequality than many of her peers at the college, most of whom were younger and had not traveled abroad. Probably she often talked about this with me because she sensed that it was something I could understand from my own, different but related, experiences as a woman in both American and Japanese cultures.

While our both being women bonded us and seemed to promote greater mutuality and thus a greater feeling of well-being, it also made for a lot of shared cultural assumptions, which I felt placed high expectations and unreasonable demands on our ability to understand unspoken communication between us. Although this did not at first appear to pose a problem, later diary entries show that such assumptions were at times problematic, in that cases of miscommunication may have created some tension between us.

Even though Akemi was a student at the university at which I taught, differences in age did not at first

seem noticeable because, as she mentions in the diary
entry below, she was cast in the role of "older sister" in
school, as well as at home, which made her act
maturely. She also often expressed concern and, to
some degree, anxiety, at the various ways people are
situated as "inside" or "outside" her culture.

Since we often talked about women and men, gender cut across other social boundaries. When we talked
about school, or Japanese and American culture, however, our positions shifted slightly, as it became more
obvious that Akemi was a Japanese student and I was
an American teacher.

In the following diary entry I describe my initial
impressions of Akemi during my first tutoring sessions
with her.

February 10

Akemi is a 24-year-old student at Lehman/
Hiroshima college. She is about 5′4″ tall, has
short, straight black hair, big, dark-brown eyes,
and a very pretty, expressive face. She is of
medium build, athletic looking; I feel small next to
her. Her clothing reflects a casual but comfortable
lifestyle. She wears a little makeup and usually one
earring in each ear, despite the fact that she has
three holes in each ear—a very unusual sight on
Japanese women. (She had her ears pierced in the
United States.) She went to the United States after
graduating high school in Japan, and got an associate degree at a community college in Oregon.
During that time, she became fluent in English,
lived by herself, and had an American boyfriend.
She says that her stay in the United States
changed her from a "real shy Japanese girl" to a
more outgoing and brave individual. She is very
friendly and active with the American students at
the college and devotes a lot of her time to tutoring
them in Japanese. I am the only faculty member to

whom she teaches Japanese. Since she is older than most of the students, she is viewed by some of her Japanese male friends as an "older sister" to whom people go with problems, which she has mildly complained to me about, but she sees this role as a social obligation to her classmates, whom she describes as *wakai* [young]. We planned to meet 2 hours a week, since that is all the time either one of us have available at this point.

My self-perception as "small" in comparison to Akemi seems significant given the fact that Akemi was only 2 inches taller and slightly larger-framed than me. One of the things that could have contributed to my feeling small in relation to Akemi was that she spoke to me as if she were speaking to a child. Simplified forms of language such as those Akemi used with me are referred to in the literature on second-language acquisition as "motherese," or "foreigner talk" (Snow & Ferguson, 1977) and are considered to be types of "caretaking" speech. However, I experienced "foreigner talk" as a conflict: on the one hand, the adjustments and simplifications Akemi made were a comfort in that I did not have to strain to understand her; on the other hand, being spoken down to may have contributed to my having felt reduced.

Feb. 16

I met Akemi today at 4:30 at our usual place, the second-floor faculty lounge. This area is furnished with a couch, a low table, TV, and a small kitchen area. It is the most "homey" room in the building. I like sitting in there, except for when other faculty members walk in and out. This makes me feel self-conscious. I began by telling her that I want to practice both writing and speaking. Last time we spent the whole time writing, which I found very tedious. Akemi began with writing. She told me to write my address and explained how to write the *kanji* as I wrote. During that time I didn't speak much, but I understood what she was saying. There are gaps on the tape when neither one of us is speaking. Since my writing is much weaker than my speaking, she might think I need to work on this. Listening to the tape, I hear myself nervously giggling. I probably felt embarrassed by my terrible handwriting and overwhelmed by all the *kanji.* Akemi's voice is lively and she also laughs a lot, which helps me feel more comfortable. When she speaks to me it sounds as if she is talking to a child. I was practicing Chiyoda-*cho* [-town] and Hiroshima-*ken* [-prefecture]. She suggested that we go on, but at that point—it had been 20 minutes— I said I wanted to practice speaking also. She said okay, but told me to finish writing my address first. She had me write Yamagata-*gun* [county]. I didn't talk at all while writing this *kanji.* I was getting tired of writing, and thought it was a waste of time to do this with her since I can practice writing on my own (even though I don't). When I finished I laughed and said, a little more assertively, "No more *kanji.*" She laughed and we switched into conversation.

Then I looked through a Japanese textbook I had brought, *Beginning Japanese Part II,* to find a chapter to talk about. I stopped at a picture of a festival. I spoke in very short, simple sentences. Akemi did most of the talking, explaining about festivals. I didn't mind listening because I am still at the stage where I need to do a lot of listening. Akemi speaks very clearly and smoothly. My pronunciation sounds American and broken. She is very expressive. When she doesn't understand, she wriggles her nose and makes funny faces. When she is interested in something her eyes become enormous. Akemi described the picture—identifying certain dances, shops, and clothing. I would have liked her to ask me some questions, but instead I asked her questions relating to festivals: "Have you ever been to Gion *matsuri* [festival]? Chiyoda *matsuri?*" And so on. She gave lengthy answers, explaining the historical background of festivals. I asked her if she likes history. She said that she did. I asked her what courses she is taking and what her major is. She said her major is economics. When I asked her why she is studying at this college she said, first of all, because it is close to her hometown, and since she is a daughter—*choojo* [firstborn daughter]—her parents want her to come home every weekend. She also taught me the words for the eldest son [*choonan*], which are different from *musume* [daughter] and *musuko* [son], words that do not qualify the birth order. She also told me that she has two younger brothers, and that the *choonan* is studying at a university in Nagasaki, which she said was a very good school. She explained the traditional custom of men being more important in the families. She said her parents are very worried about her and don't want her to go to New York. (I'm not sure why her parents are so protective of her now, when she is 24, since they sent her to America to study for 2 years when she was 18.)

She went on to explain the traditional custom of taking baths in the family—men first, then women. She said her family doesn't follow the tradition—people bathe whenever they want, and she seemed proud of the fact that her father cooks and her mother sleeps later than her father. She added, though, that her father sometimes says "bad things" to her and her mother like, "But you are a woman." But she explained this away by saying it was because "he was born before the war." She also told me that she was born in the year of the cock, which is this year, and that her mother was too. She said her mother was 24 when she had had her, Akemi's age. I asked her if she thought that was young. She said her mother got married right after college, and at that time it was considered old. I asked her what her mother had studied in college. She said, *"Kateka"* [home economics]. She said her mother hadn't liked it, but she had been told by her mother that was all she was allowed to study since she was going to be a housewife. I asked Akemi if she wants to get married, and she said that all of her friends where she lives are married, so . . . (she also wants to get married).

I thought about myself when I was 24, when I came to Japan for the first time, and all my friends were getting married. I asked her if her parents pressure her to get married. She said they told her, "It's okay if you want to wait until you're 40." They just worry about who will take care of her when she is old. Toward the end of the hour Akemi said, *"Onna no ho ga ii desu ne."* [Women are better than men, aren't they?] *"So desu, ne,"* I agreed. Although I didn't talk very much, I enjoyed our conversation more today than the last time.

When interacting with Akemi I laughed more than I had with Keio. One possible reason for the difference could have been because Akemi laughed more often than Keio, and I found it contagious. Akemi's laughter seemed to be a way of showing involvement and empathy. That I laughed, even when I didn't know why, suggests that, as with Keio, laughing was a way of sharing, even when there was no understanding. However, the "nervous giggles" I described sounded like the way people who do not expect to be taken seriously laugh when they try to be serious—an expression of embarrassment and discomfort, from feeling "dumb." This also could have been an expression I absorbed from my environment, since I found that Japanese people (especially women) tended to laugh a lot.

Even though Akemi did most of the talking, I did not experience feelings of being dominated, as I had with Keio. Akemi was highly verbal, but she remained consistently tuned in to whether or not I was with her. Further, as is obvious from all the questions I asked her, I was clearly interested in, and felt I had more control over, what we were talking about. This may have also been because Akemi and I often talked about topics that concerned me and that I often thought of myself. For example, in the diary entry above, it seems I had forgotten I was speaking Japanese when Akemi began to talk about her role as the firstborn daughter in her family. Although her family situation is quite different from mine, there were some things with which I felt I could identify. As I noted at the end of the entry, Akemi's experience of feeling pressured to marry corresponded to how I felt 8 years earlier, when I was her age and had been living in Japan.

Pressure on Japanese women to marry is still strong enough to cause many who choose to remain single to leave their communities, and even Japan; however, there is an easing up of parental pressure, which seems to be one of the strongest factors influencing young women's decision to wait longer before getting married. One possible explanation may have to do with increased life expectancy in Japan. Unlike the situation of the previous generation, parents in their 50s and 60s do not feel as threatened by the possibility of dying before seeing their grandchildren; and they are also not as dependent on having a daughter-in-law to care for them in their old age.

Although she felt pressured to return to her parents' home every weekend, that Akemi lived in her own apartment reveals that independence is a goal more women in Japan these days are trying to achieve. While many mothers may still explicitly laud the traditional role of wife and mother for their daughters, through their own feelings and behaviors they may be sending subliminal mixed messages to their daughters. However, other forms of social control such as conformity in schools and at the workplace make "autonomy" difficult to achieve in Japan, as it is everywhere else.

As mentioned above, the lack of privacy in the public faculty-lounge inhibited me to some extent; however, I did not feel as great a need to seek out places outside of the college, such as my apartment or coffee shops, to study with Akemi as I had with Keio, with whom I seemed to be much more conscious of the physical environment.

Unlike the rigid boundaries I experienced with Keio, which made me feel blocked off and distanced from him emotionally, Akemi's personal stories, vivid details, imagery, and concreteness, helped to draw me in. This helped me to feel more connected to her. Even though Akemi was often more talkative than I, I always felt that she was highly aware of my participation as a listener: she was attentive to my nonverbal messages, such as eye contact, smiles, and head nods, and could tell whether I was with her or in another world, which was not often the case with Keio.

As our dialogue became more authentic and less contrived I felt there was a simultaneous easing up of role restraints. My resistance to Akemi's instruction in the beginning of the diary entry above may reflect my resistance to her playing a role as "teacher," for the less she did so, the more willing I seemed to ask questions and to lead the conversation in a certain direction. Movement from feeling tight and constrained to open and relaxed can also be observed in the way I wrote my diary. In the beginning, when our roles were static and the focus was on form and structure, my writing appears disembodied and fragmented; however, in the latter half of the entry, when the focus shifts to content, my sentences appear to be longer and my thoughts fuller, more complete. Such patterns could also be seen in our relationship: when the relationship was distant and unconnected, communication became skeletal; when I perceived mutuality and connectedness, there seemed to be a corresponding feeling of extending, responding more fully, sharing more of myself. There are important implications here for language learning, in that feeling connected to another person helps to motivate a learner to want to talk to him or her; whereas, experiencing no such connection often makes communication (even among people who speak the same language) strained and difficult.

In the previous chapter we saw how Keio's non-interactive approach of directly translating words from a dictionary tended to alienate me from what I was reading. The details provided below of a reading lesson with Akemi show how an interactive approach to reading was much more facilitative.

Feb. 23

I began reading. I noticed my reading has sped up a bit from when I first began reading this book. Two children came in and made a lot of noise. I can hardly hear myself on the tape. I couldn't concentrate on what I was reading. I was just reading the words. When I finished, Akemi asked if I understood what I had read. I said (in Japanese), "Not at all. I couldn't concentrate with all this noise." She agreed. Then she said, "Let's read it one more time." She read it to me and explained every line in Japanese. She spoke clearly, stretching out the pronunciation of some words. This was helpful since it is hard for me to hear long sounds. I was aware of her exaggerating them and I didn't repeat them this way. She gave lots of hypothetical examples, using names of people at the college and of things that I or she might do. For example, when explaining the word to talk to oneself—*hitorigoto*—

she said, "Karen-*san wa hitori de sundeimasu kara tokidoki hitorigoto suru deshyoo*" [You live alone, so you probably talk to yourself sometimes]. She said that she does it because she is lonely, vividly and humorously reenacting a scene when she talks to herself. Sometimes she went into lengthy explanations, which I found difficult to follow, but when I slipped out of concentration she noticed and would bring me back with, "*Daijobu?*" [Okay?]. For the last ten minutes I suggested that we practice using some of the new words in conversation, so we went through the pages, looking for words I hadn't known and used them in sentences.

Whereas Keio seemed to privilege correctness over understanding, Akemi clearly put more energy into conveying meaning. Her vivid and creative dramatization of scenes, her stories, and her humor helped me gain more confidence in my ability to understand in Japanese, without having to rely on English translations. Indeed, Akemi was very theatrical. She acted out words and expressions, attended to illustrations, and referred to familiar, concrete people and places outside of the text, which greatly contributed to my ability to comprehend the text in Japanese. Also in contrast to what I experienced as Keio's rigid and unyielding style, I experienced Akemi as nurturing and generous, which helped make learning Japanese with her much more pleasurable for me. Her high degree of verbal involvement, easily understandable speech, willingness to repeat and to paraphrase, provide examples, make things clear, as well as her wide-range of paralinguistic facilitators such as animated facial expressions, laughter, nods, and eye contact gave me a lot more opportunities to understand her. The entry below provides some examples of some of the ways Akemi's affirming approach made me feel more positive about my language ability, even when I made mistakes.

March 19

I seem to be having problems with the particles *ni* and *no*. For example, I asked her, *"Nani wa ii karada ga ii tabemono wa nan desu ka?"* [What are healthy foods?] I asked if that was correct. *"Karada ni ii mono,"* she corrected. "You got 80 percent right." After a few self-corrections, Akemi said, *"Wakarimashita"* [I understand].

I pulled out my journal and asked her to correct what I had written. She pointed out some ambiguous sentences and some grammar mistakes. I was disappointed to see that I had made so many mistakes. I think she picked up on this because she said that the students studying Japanese would be happy to be at my level. She tried to give me some encouragement. Then she helped me write a new journal entry. . . .

She lent me some folk stories that she said she read in about the third or forth grade. I am finding them quite challenging. I read out-loud and Akemi explained. The problem with these stories is the language—a lot of the words are not used in conversation, so I've never heard them before. When Akemi explains the meaning of the sentences in different words, I can understand them easily. I'm enjoying the stories, though. Akemi is an excellent tutor. She is very patient and encouraging. Even though it takes me forever to get through one sentence she responds positively when I finish it—unlike Keio, who seems to grow impatient much more easily. She is very verbal—gives lengthy explanations and can come up with a lot of examples when it takes me a while to catch on. She also has a good sense of humor. Yesterday we were talking about our plans for the weekend. She asked me if I was going on the trip this weekend. I said yes. Then she asked what day it was today, and

answered herself, "Thursday." I asked if her English teacher had told her. She looked at me with her
eyes wide open and asked incredulously, "Did she
tell me what day it is?" Of course I was talking
about the trip, not what day today was. I laughed
because I thought she was making a joke. However,
I wonder if it was really a misunderstanding.
Although I'm feeling more comfortable with Akemi,
I became very inhibited when other teachers
walked into the room. I noticed myself clam up. I
don't know why, but I feel uncomfortable speaking
Japanese in front of other American teachers.

Commentary that appears repeatedly in my diary
deals with feeling self-conscious while speaking Japanese in front of other American teachers. Changing roles
from English teacher to Japanese learner was complicated: in a sense it displaced me from a position of privilege and divided me from other American teachers,
most of whom did not speak Japanese. The anxiety
underlying what I described in my diary as "shyness"
and "inhibition" could have been at least in part due to
my reluctance at showing a kind of superiority—lording
over those who were not trying to make the effort to
learn Japanese. It may have also been at least partially
brought about by a fear of exposing, through the protective covering of my role as English teacher, what I
feared might be my naked incompetence as a language
learner. My position as teacher at the university made
me feel a peculiar tug of loyalty between American
teachers and Japanese students. The tension reveals a
conflict—of both wanting and not wanting to move out
of a certain space. It also suggests that I was operating
under an assumption that a bond existed between me
and other teachers, separating "us" from "them"—the
students; and that by separating myself from other
teachers, I was somehow violating this assumption, as
lines of authority between us became compromised. In

some sense, I was betraying my somewhat privileged place in an oppressive hierarchy.

The way Akemi talks about herself in relation to other Japanese women in the entry below is similarly revealing of ways in which language is influenced by our interests in enjoying certain privileges in society. We see in Akemi's discussion of Japanese women below, how placing oneself "inside" a culture often comes at the expense of others, who are targeted as the "outsiders."

March 26

Akemi begins by asking me, "What should we do today?" I respond by saying I didn't plan anything. We both think for a moment and then she suggests, "How about conversation?" I agree. She waits for me to initiate the conversation, and it takes me a few minutes to come up with something. Finally I say that I like her sweater. It was very bright and colorful. I say that I heard that Japanese people don't like to draw attention to themselves by wearing such bright colors. She listens without responding at first and then corrects me as I speak. I tell her about the time when I wore my very colorful tie-dyed Betsy Johnson dress in the Imperial Hotel in Tokyo where I was waiting for a friend and overheard two elderly women in the women's room say that my dress was *hade* [gaudy]. I understood what it meant and it made me feel very self-conscious about wearing a "gaudy"-looking dress. Akemi explains that Japanese prefer *jimi* [plain] clothes because others will laugh at them if they wear clothes that are too bright. She says that if her grandmother wore a red dress she would be laughed at. She uses the passive voice, which I remembered from my class, and I ask if it was the passive, but Akemi doesn't seem to understand my question, so I just continue with the conversation.

Akemi says that she likes a variety of colors. Sometimes she wears white, sometimes other colors. She asks me about the clothes I like. As I talked about what kinds of and what color clothes I liked I noticed that the length of my sentences seemed to be getting longer.

Then Akemi began to make fun of Japanese people. She got into a discussion of *buriko* [girlish] women. She said she didn't like women who acted this way just to impress men. I asked her why she thought they did that. She said she didn't know—maybe because they are *baka* [fools]. I laughed. She asked me what I thought. I said I thought she was right. I asked her about her 2½ years in the United States—Had she kept a journal? She said she hadn't, but she still remembered. She said she had changed a lot when she lived in the United States. I asked her in what ways. She said that she had changed from being a "typical shy Japanese girl" and that she had became less *hazukashii* [shy, reserved]. She said she had talked to a lot of people, and asked questions when she didn't understand things.

More than other times, I asked her to repeat words I didn't understand. She suggested that when I didn't understand something I interrupt her by saying, *"Chotto matte!"* [Just a minute]. I was enjoying the time and felt energized by our discussion. (I am usually so tired by the end of the day.) She talked about her mother, telling me about how she had "corrected" her when Akemi had come home from the United States—mostly table manners. She also explained that Japanese aren't *kichen* [clear]; they don't say what they are really thinking; they always just respond, *"Hai!"* [Yes!]. Americans, in contrast, she explained, "clearly say what they think," and when she came back to Japan she didn't like the way people didn't say what they thought. I asked her why people don't say what they think, and she said it was because groups in Japan are very strong, and that people don't want to be on the outside, so they conform to the behavior of the whole group. Then she asked me if I clearly said what I thought. I said I try to but don't always. She also complained about having to speak *teinei* [politely] to "important" people. I asked her what people would be "important." She said the president of the college, some teachers, older people. I asked her if she speaks differently to me than to her friends. She said no—but sometimes she uses *kitanai* [dirty] Japanese with her friends. She said that my Japanese is *kirei* [pretty, clean]—that I don't use *kitanai* Japanese. Akemi called herself *urusai* [loud, noisy]—she said she is "noisy" when she speaks Japanese, but "quiet" when she speaks English.

At the end of the hour I began to get tired, but the time went by fast, and I was clearly engaged in this conversation. I asked her at the end what she thought of this way of studying Japanese. She said if it was good for me, then she thought it was good. I expressed concern that I make a lot of mistakes when I speak, and asked her if she would correct me when I did. She said that she didn't hear me make many mistakes. I asked her if my level of politeness was appropriate for our conversation. She said my Japanese is polite, the kind of speech that is comforting for people to hear. She imitated the way some men speak, saying how "scary" it sounds. She says at home she sometimes speaks in this "rough, slang" speech and her mother corrects her by saying, "Speak *onna rashiku*" [like a woman]. She says she responds to such commands unenthusiastically and her mother tells her to respond obediently, by saying *"Hai!"*

I looked at my watch and said, "It's time, isn't

it?" It was 5 minutes before 5. She has a class at 5. Then, unexpectedly, she began to imitate her economics teacher. I laughed, but began to feel uncomfortable as she listed all the "strange" things he does. *"Kare wa honto ni okashii yo!"* [He is really strange!] I tried to defend him by saying (in Japanese): "Well, I'm sure he is very good at economics." She made a face. And then went on about how odd he looks when he is running and exercising. She stressed that *everyone* says so. I began to get paranoid and said, "The students probably enjoy making fun of all the teachers." She said that the only ones the students don't like are her economics teacher and one of her English teachers, who is also a man. The latter, she said, "no one" likes because he always smells of garlic. I tried to tell her seriously that I didn't think she should be telling me these things about her teachers. She asked me why not. I said because I am a teacher here at this college and it is not "professional." Then she said, "Okay, let's be professional." This made me laugh again.

Moving through the entry, I first notice Akemi's hesitation in response to my comment about liking her colorful sweater (correcting me instead of responding). This seems interesting, since compliments in Japanese often serve the opposite practical function that they do in English: to express indirectly an insult or complaint. Similar to the function of politeness, compliments in Japanese may be a distancing strategy, or a way to "encode social distinctions" (Wetzel, 1994, 79). In effect, the function is another way of marking "insider" and "outsider" boundaries. Not knowing what a person is really saying when she or he expresses a compliment requires a standard rejection: *"Iie, sono koto wa arimasen"* [Oh no, not at all], which is usually followed by a form of self-effacement ("It is really very old"; "It's cheap"; "It makes me look fat"). The rejection, on the one hand "saves face" by projecting modesty, a personality trait highly valued in Japan, and thus situates one as inside the culture. Accepting a compliment, by saying "Thank you," on the other hand, smacks of self-indulgence, egocentrism, and even ignorance in the ears of Japanese traditionalists, most of whom believe adults should speak from *tatemae* [what is socially acceptable] rather than *honne* [one's true feelings]. For example, the expression *"Nihongo wa o-jyozu desu ne"* [Your Japanese is very good], is often lavished on foreigners who can just barely utter a few words. The ability to interpret this expression, not at face value, but rather, as "I know it is very difficult for you to speak Japanese, and I appreciate your effort," may in fact be a first step toward really understanding Japanese. Akemi's hesitation in response to my compliment may have reflected the conflict of, on the one hand, having to put herself down and, on the other, risking appearing immodest, ignorant, and quite possibly, not Japanese.

Just as speech-acts function pragmatically to situate people inside or outside a group, scrutinizing people's appearances is also a way of objectifying people, separating "them" from "us." The terms *hade* [gaudy] and *jimi* [plain] operate as a type of control mechanism that regulates the way people are supposed to look. The fact that people are not only noticed for wearing red dresses but are "laughed at" signals an alarm that people (women) are supposed to look a certain way so as not to call attention to their selfhood. This leads one to wonder, who are the people the Japanese do not want to look like, and what does this mean? (And when and why did Akemi's grandmother want to wear a red dress?)

As a white-skinned, red-haired foreigner in Japan, I could hardly avoid being noticed wherever I went. There are some foreigners—namely, Asian immigrants—who live a shadowy existence in Japanese society; in fact, some people might even think they do not exist. The question this raises is not why nobody sees them—for clearly they are seen by each other—but, rather, who doesn't see them and why?

In recent years there has been a strong push from the government toward "internationalism" in Japan; however, behind the propaganda there are actual forms of discrimination against certain foreigners. The word *gaijin* is used even for non-native Japanese who are born in Japan but are required to carry fingerprinted "alien" registration cards with them at all times.

The work many Asian immigrants do is in great demand by Japanese citizens: they run the entertainment and gambling businesses such as the ubiquitous *pachinko* parlors; they are employed as prostitutes, domestic workers, farmers, and factory employees. However, they are still treated as outsiders in Japanese society. Even the non-Japanese who died as a result of the atomic bomb are not listed with the Japanese victims on the memorial inside Hiroshima Peace Park. Instead, a separate memorial for Korean victims is located outside the park.

I am struck by a marked absence in my diary: there is no reference of any kind to my being Jewish. Most Japanese people assumed I was Christian and I did very little to make it clear that I wasn't. Admittedly, my secular background contributes to my ambivalence toward religion. However, it is likely that the complete silence surrounding my Jewishness was a response to something that I internalized from my environment—a similar sense of negation or invalidation that some of the "foreigners" who are assumed to be invisible may feel. Underlying this silence seems to be a desire to fit in, and not be further marked as something one is not supposed to be.

A different, but related, example of my closeting a part of my identity can be observed in my reaction to how Akemi perceived (or pretended to perceive) my age:

April 2

   Akemi asked me how old I was. I asked her
what she thought. She said she thought I was in
my 20s, around 27. I said older. She asked tenta-
tively if I was 30. I didn't want to shock her too
much, so I said yes. She widened her eyes, let out
a big *Bikkurishita!* [Oh my God!], and said that I
didn't look 30. I thought she must think I am
ancient. I was glad I didn't tell her that I am really
32.

   Earlier, I said that age did not seem to be a significant difference between Akemi and me. However, that
I reduced my age in the exchange above led me to consider that age did in fact matter. My being seen as
young seems significant, but even more important is
that being young (and Christian) were perceived—by
both Akemi and me—as positive.

   I experienced feelings of mutuality in my relationship with Akemi, which I perceived to be helpful in
learning Japanese with her. The exchange above shows
how tenuous and volatile this "mutuality" can be. What
becomes clearer in retrospect is that I may have felt a
connection to her that may not have existed because I
needed to make contact. Yet, even though I may have
felt it, I didn't trust it, or perhaps I was scared of losing
it. Another example of this phenomenon could be seen
in our shared laughter in the entry above, when I joined
her in making fun of Japanese culture.

   When Akemi called *buriko* ["girlish"] Japanese
women *baka* [fools], I laughed. Now, this laughter raises
in me a lot of questions: Did I feel pleasure at making
fun of women who behaved in certain ways just to get
men's attention? Did I feel in solidarity with Akemi's
need to free herself from an oppressive cultural expectation? Was my laughter a way of sharing or creating a
connection with Akemi? Or, did I feel a cultural superiority to these women, to the kinds of accommodations

they were making with their culture, as if somehow I could be sure that, if I were in their place, I wouldn't act in a similar way? How possibly was my laughter different from Akemi's? Could I perhaps have been laughing *at*, rather than *with*, her?

My laughter and silence in response to Akemi's making fun of her teachers raises even more questions: What is going on in situations when sharing and connectedness are desired, but when we are in fact not sharing the same assumptions? And, why did I laugh more easily at Japanese than at Americans?

My conflicted response—of discomfort on the one hand, and understanding on the other—raises still more questions: Why did I feel the need to defend these teachers? Was it because they were colleagues, and think it was a professional betrayal to go on listening to her negative comments about them? Or was it because they were Jewish, and, on some subliminal level, I picked up messages of anti-Semitism? Even more important, what bothered Akemi about these men? And what bothered me about Keio? Was it a certain weakness that we perceived in them that made us feel threatened or uncomfortable? Strangely enough, it seems that the very thing that made us feel powerful in relation to them made us want to take a kind of gender revenge on them. The irony in this is that by scapegoating men who, at least in this one way, were vulnerable, we played into the "masculinized" image of men and, at the same time, reproduced our own oppression—by co-constructing our "feminized" identities—and thus, ultimately, used our own power against ourselves.

In spite of calling "men's" language crude, dirty, noisy, and scary, and "women's" language beautiful and correct, Akemi expressed a preference to speak the male version. Her descriptions of self as "quiet" in English and "noisy" in Japanese reveal that she is aware of stepping in and out of different personas in order to adjust to the changing cultural perceptions others had of her in different contexts. Even though she said she felt less shy in the United States, she seemed to have internalized an image of herself there as a quiet, perhaps even submissive, Japanese woman; in Japan, her view of self as loud and noisy might be a reflection of being seen by some Japanese as a cultural hybrid—due to the influence of her overseas experience and her expertise in English. The femininity training and corrections Akemi received from her mother when she returned from the United States clearly convey her mother's anxiety about Akemi being perceived as a *gaijin* in her own culture.

The tendency to resist traditional female language seems to be growing among young, modern Japanese woman. By presenting themselves in opposition to the feminine model, some women can challenge boundaries they find constricting. This raises a problem, however, similar to what many of us are faced with. How can we move out of an imposed language without acquiring the oppressor's language? How can we "empower" ourselves without either reproducing or integrating ourselves into oppressive structures of power and domination? I think Audre Lorde provided deep insight into this problem when she wrote, "The master's tools will never dismantle the master's house."

Hegemony occurs as people get caught up in complying with cultural tendencies that contribute to their own oppression, such as by means of self-censorship. In Akemi's case, speaking an "illegitimate" form of language is done to resist dominance; however, in trying to minimize the difference, she may be perpetuating the dominance. This is a problem that is difficult to eradicate because it is a general belief that in order to get power one must associate with it, which often means learning how to speak like those in power.

Acting in complicity with one's own oppressor has been described in a number of ways by different social researchers (Bourdieu, 1977; de Beauvior, 1952; Foucault, 1980). Susan Gal (1991) uses the term "symbolic domination," and articulates the central idea as follows:

> The control of discourse or of representations of reality occurs in social interaction, located in institutions, and is a source of social power; it may be, therefore, the occasion for coercion, conflict, or complicity. (p. 177)

In the previous chapter I described, on the one hand, feeling "outside," and thus restrained and controlled, in relation to Keio, even when I was in my own apartment. With Akemi, on the other hand, I felt I could be "at home," and express myself more openly and spontaneously, even when we were at the university. The diary entry below strongly suggests that, in addition to age and social status, economics played an important role in situating me "inside" the interaction.

April 5

> . . . I was annoyed at Akemi yesterday for showing up late again. When she arrived about 15 minutes late I told her that she always comes late. She was very apologetic and said that she is always rushing to get here. When I went up to the college this morning I found a note written in Japanese—mostly *hiragana* [phonetic alphabet] and simple *kanji*—from Akemi. She apologized profusely for coming late and left a bag of oranges and three Japanese children's books on my desk. I was able to read the whole note, except for some parts that were written in *katakana* [alphabet for foreign words], which I had some problems understanding.

Unlike my experience with Keio, with whom I engaged in a language-exchange rather than paid tutoring-sessions, my relationship with Akemi had an economic dimension that seems to have given me more freedom to express how I felt. Money symbolized power by giving me a voice that counted. Relationships that are based on money, such as those between clients and therapists, publishers and writers, and so on, often have unclear parameters since they are neither friendships nor purely business affiliations. Although a strong bond often develops due to the intimate nature of the relationship, money clearly adds a dimension of power in which the time individuals spend together is often believed to be "owned" by the person paying.

What seems most striking in the above entry is the way Akemi seemed to capitulate so easily to my anger. This leads me to wonder if my anger frightened her. Perhaps the directness and tone in which I expressed myself represented male anger—which she described elsewhere as "scary." In which case, she may have responded both to her association of male anger and to my replication of it. In the previous chapter I discussed how being in a relationship in which my feelings were not regarded made me not only contain them but also feel ashamed and guilty for having such feelings. Although in my diary I did not identify my feelings toward Keio—who also not only came late, but sometimes did not even show up—as anger, it seems that anger indeed underlay much of my frustration, disappointment, boredom, and ambivalence.

Akemi may have been similarly silenced in her relationship with me. For example, a comment she made about anger not long after the above incident seems very revealing: "Japanese people don't show their anger. They keep it inside. They don't say what they really feel or think, but inside they complain a lot." When I asked Akemi if she ever gets angry, she responded, unequivocally, "No." The entry below illustrates how she refuses to claim her anger, even when it is highly justifiable:

April 11

I asked her if she is planning to graduate from this college or finish at the Bronx campus. She said she was forced to go to the New York campus since this college isn't offering her major anymore. I asked her how she felt about that. She said her mother was very angry.

Another time, however, Akemi told me that she once got so angry at her brother, she threw something at him, causing his head to bleed profusely. This leads me to wonder not whether a person of another culture gets angry—clearly we all do—but rather, how do we express anger differently in different contexts and why? And, if suppressed anger leads to violence, what does this mean for people who are marginalized and oppressed due to gender, race, class, and other social injustices?

Clearly, these questions have serious political implications in that they point to the relationship between language and power on the one hand, and the construction of cultural identities on the other. When a person is situated "outside" a culture, she or he becomes more controlled by the social context and detached from what she or he is feeling and thinking; conversely, a person who is "inside," can be more spontaneous, engaged, relaxed, and connected to her or his feelings. As power relations shift from one context to another, so do people's perceptions of how much they have to adjust to other people's norms.

Although Akemi's speech was not weak or lacking authority, her nurturing and caretaking quality, which increased my comfort and facilitated my process of learning to speak in Japanese, ironically reinforced what some gender researchers have identified as features of "women's" or "powerless" language (Lakoff, 1970; Spender, 1980). I believed I was sensitive to the workings of power in language; however, my interactions with Akemi is telling of the ways in which women—even those who consider themselves feminists—participate in the construction of their own and other women's oppression. In taking Akemi's "invisible" linguistic work for granted, I may have been reproducing the very things that dominance theorists argue burden women in social interactions.

In retrospect, I see that the anger I unleashed at Akemi may have been a misguided shot, one that may have been intended for Keio. This reveals the unfortunate phenomenon of targeting the wrong people: those who hurt us the least, and to whom we feel powerful in relation. Do the people with whom we most closely identify most often end up being the recipients of our abuse? Akemi's strong reaction to my telling her that she always came late suggests that she may have felt I was putting her in her place and implying that she was cheating me out of some of the time for which I was paying; hence, the gifts. The event unfortunately created a loss of a quality I found endearing in Akemi—her spontaneity—and could have even severed the one common bond we had, as women. Once again, we see gender not as something fixed but as relative to a particular context—a relationship that involves constant dialogue with another person. Understanding gender requires the ability to see beyond biological differences, to the symbolic sense of the concept—as part of a wider social, political, economic, cultural, and ideological means of stratification.

There were other parallels in how Akemi related to me and how I related to Keio. Notice, for example, how in a similar way to what I had attempted with Keio, Akemi seems to have been making more of an attempt to establish "intimacy" when we were in my apartment.

April 15

Last night Akemi came over at about 8:30 and stayed until 10 p.m. She brought two boxes of cookies. I made coffee, and we sat on my couch and talked in Japanese the whole time. We talked about ourselves and other people a lot. She began, as usual, making fun of her teachers, particularly one of her English teachers. She went on and on about how he smells of garlic. She said when she leaves his class she has to go get some fresh air. She complained also that he laughs and gets angry at his students when they make mistakes. I am doing more listening than speaking in the beginning, and am following everything she says pretty well. This time I confided to her that I don't like him very much either. I especially disliked him yesterday, since my coordinator told me that he complained that I didn't show up to a meeting he held, which he never bothered to tell me about!

Eventually I changed the subject by asking her a lot of questions about her time in America. She said when she went there she was "a real Japanese girl." I asked her what she meant by that. She gave me a few examples. For one, when she lived with her host family during the first 3 weeks she didn't know how to say "No thank you" when they offered her food, so she just kept taking whatever they offered her whether she wanted it or not. She said this caused her to gain a lot of weight. I told her the same thing had happened to me the first time I lived in Japan. She also talked about her trouble with English. She carried a dictionary around with her at all times. She also told me about her American boyfriend whom she hasn't seen—or heard from—for 3 years (but apparently still thinks of as her "boyfriend"). She asked me if I have a boyfriend and I said no. I said that I had been seeing someone, but we had split up before I came to Japan. She looked at me very sympathetically. I also felt a little sorry for myself.

Then we talked about schools, comparing

Japanese and American teachers and school systems. She told me horror stories of how she was
punished in school by being made to sit *seiza* [on
her knees] on a hard floor for 3 hours, and by being
hit on the head with sticks and having chalk
thrown at her by her teachers—for breaking the
school rules. I told her how surprised I had been to
see this kind of violence when I taught in Japanese
junior-high schools. She talked about her 18-year-
old brother, who has been going to school in
Nagasaki since he was about 13 "because he is
smart and it is a very good school." She said she
feels sorry for him because all he ever does is
study. She said that she and her other brother are
different from this brother. They prefer to talk and
have fun with their friends rather than to study. We
just kept talking and the time went by very fast.
Before I knew it, it was 10 p.m. and I felt guilty that
I had kept her for so long. I thanked her for staying
and invited her to come over again. Then I offered
to pay her, but she said no, that she is doing it
because she is my friend. That was sweet, but I still
insisted on paying her for the extra 2 hours.

There were certain things Akemi did that made our
interaction in my apartment seem more intimate than
the interactions that took place at the university. For
example, bringing cookies, taking off her shoes, talking
about her feelings, especially bad ones, as well as refus-
ing to be paid—all contributed to anchoring Akemi in
more of an *uchi* [intimate] context. Our personal, intimate way of speaking seems to be a type of "female
genre," and a benign tactic used, in both directions, as
a means to smooth social boundaries. However, like
everything else, "intimacy" cannot be viewed as a neutral concept, either in Japanese or in English, because
within the same social context intimacy has different
meanings for different individuals, depending on where

they stand in relation to power. For example, intimacy may be used as a way for a person in power to allow another to open up or feel comfortable; however, the person being controlled may feel vulnerable, since her personal information can be used against her. Being intimate, depending on where one stands in the hierarchy, might be interpreted as a violation of privacy, even a form of exploitation: a person may want to be intimate with someone in order to seduce her or him. While people in power may actually try to humanize a situation by inviting intimacy from subordinates, it is not the same when intimacy goes the other way. When the person in the lower position invites or initiates intimacy with a person in a higher position her or his gesture may be misinterpreted (or correctly interpreted) as ingratiating.

In English, too, there are different ways I speak to people, as my place in the hierarchy shifts from one context to another. For example, I speak to students differently than I speak to teachers and administrators. Whereas with the former I can often be relaxed, the situation with the latter often feels more formal and constraining. Where a person stands in the hierarchy has a lot to do with how she or he speaks, acts, even feels. People in power authorize what can be talked about where, when, and how.

Akemi's experience with weight gain in the United States reminded me of my first year in Japan. I gained 15 kilograms. As I recall, I was constantly being fed. Although I liked the food, there were other reasons why I seemed to consume ravenously everything I was offered: there is a connection between food and language. They are both primal needs, expressed and fulfilled orally. I so much wanted to take in, feel, taste, and enjoy the new language and culture; I could do so by eating it. Food gave me a way to communicate, share pleasurable experiences, and feel a sense of commonality. Where I was starved for words, food satisfied my hunger. Food offered a universal connection; it was the sustenance of relationships.

Akemi ascribed her weight gain in the United States to her inability to say "No, thank you." I could also relate to this, as I did not always know when or how to say "yes" and "no" in Japanese. While it is not difficult learning these words, knowing when "yes" might also mean "no" and vice versa in another language requires deeper cultural understanding. Akemi's depiction of her mother telling her to respond obediently, by saying *"Hai"* [Yes!], is an example of the ways women are socialized to be compliant and placating, so as not to hurt or offend others. In a language such as Japanese, in which "yes" and "no" are often ambiguous, this cultural conditioning might pose as great a threat to women as it does in languages, such as English, where "yes" and "no" are taken more literally. Being taught to be compliant for the sake of maintaining relationships is one of the hazards of being a woman, for it reflects an absence of boundaries, a being open and unguarded for invasion and exploitation. When such invasions become pervasive and commonplace in a woman's day-to-day experiences, they are hard to notice or make much of at the time. However, these everyday acts of intrusion add up to differences in the amounts of territory men and women feel entitled to claim in social interactions.

The interaction below provides a good example of this phenomenon:

April 20

We met as usual at 3:00 in the English Language Department lounge. Usually there aren't so many people walking in and out, but today it was a busy thoroughfare. I spent the first 10 minutes of the 60-minute lesson making coffee and talking to Robert, the office manager, who was just hanging around. (This was rather annoying since I was supposed to be having a private lesson.) When I told him that we were having a private lesson he said, *"Boku mo benkyoo shitai naa"* [I want to study too] in an *amae* [childlike] voice. I was glad to hear Akemi respond that he could have a tutor for 500 yen per hour. Finally, he was called away by his work and left us alone.

For a change I had a structure to our time. Rather than just having conversation, I wanted to review the verbs for giving and receiving (*ageru* and *morau* or *kudaru*), so I practiced them by talking about giving Akemi a cup of coffee and receiving a lesson from her.

We briefly engaged in small talk. Akemi asked me if I enjoyed the other night (when she came over to my apartment). I said that I had and asked her the same question. She responded that it was *"dai-jobu"* [okay]. This seemed like a lukewarm response, but I didn't know why. She said she was able to eat first, "so . . ." I interpreted the part she left out as her telling me indirectly that if she comes over in the evening after her classes, she may be hungry. I suggested that next time we have dinner together. She agreed that this would be a good idea.

We see in this entry how even though I was "annoyed" by Robert's interruption, I indulged him in conversation and coffee for 10 minutes, which moved me out of the context of my lesson to one in which I became accommodating to him. Also interesting is Akemi's direct response to Robert, "One hour costs 500 yen," which was quite different from her indirect way of communicating with me, particularly in the way she communicated that she had been expecting to eat at my apartment.

The end of the semester marked a time of change that created increased tension and agitation in me and,

I suspect, in Akemi as well. We were both preoccupied by our preparations to leave Japan. I felt anxious about the transition and Akemi was also probably nervous about moving to New York. One of our last conversations in Japan reveals that, although I had genuinely wanted to spend time with Akemi in New York, my highly qualified invitation may have been interpreted as the exact opposite of what I consciously intended to convey.

May 17

She asked me if I would tell her my telephone number in New York. I said, *"Mochiron"* [Of course]. I asked her where she would be staying when she arrives. She said she didn't know yet. I told her she can stay in my apartment if she needs to, until she finds an apartment. I explained that there isn't much room, but if she needed a place for a while, it would be okay. She said she will arrive in New York in August. I told her that August would be a good time to contact me because I'd be much busier in September.

Although I was unaware of what it was at the time, something I had said or done seemed to have hurt Akemi, as she did not interact with me much after this exchange. She did call me, however, a couple of weeks after she arrived in New York. We met only once that summer and talked on the phone again about 6 months later. For the first time, we spoke to one another in English. She had been living in the Bronx with her American boyfriend and her brother. She told me that she "finally" got permission from her mother to stay in New York. I asked her how she did that. She said that she had "explained" her situation to her mother: that she is a woman, 25 years old, and that she has a degree from an American university; therefore, it would be difficult for her to find a good job and to live comfortably in

Japan. One of the last things she mentioned was that she had recently run into one of her American teachers in Hiroshima, the one who she had constantly complained smelled of garlic. "He's much better now," she said. "He's just like a normal American guy."

7

Satoko and Me

Since I met Keio and Akemi when I first began to reimmerse myself in Japanese, their perception of me as a beginning language learner did not seem to change as rapidly as my language ability. I met Satoko 2 months later, when my Japanese was not developing at as fast a pace. Therefore, I felt Satoko could move with me more than my other interlocutors. Further, since I was functioning at a conversational level when I met Satoko, our interactions were not focused specifically on language learning; more often, we practiced our prospective foreign languages while performing other actions, such as driving, visiting people's homes, shopping, sightseeing, or other activities of everyday living.

Although Satoko was introduced to me by Keio as a prospective language-exchange partner, our relationship developed into more of a friendship than a language-learning relationship. This may have been because I could relate to her shyness and to her self-consciousness, or perhaps to her seeming slightly out of place in the environment. As single women in our 30s, we also could relate to the pressures we perceived from our environments to get married. As many of our conversations below reflect, talking to one another may have been a way to validate or support one another in our choices to pursue other avenues besides marriage.

March 28

Yesterday while I was playing tennis, Keio walked right onto the courts to introduce me to a

new student. He told me that she would like to
learn English, and suggested that I have the same
kind of exchange with her as I have with him. I did-
n't feel I had a choice in the matter: she was standing right there. How could I have said no? He said
that she was planning to go to New York in the fall
to get a master's degree. Satoko spoke to me herself hesitantly in English with her hand covering
her mouth. This may have been because she was
wearing braces (a very unusual sight in Japan,
even on children). I asked her if she was planning
on going to New York in the fall and she responded,
"To tell you the truth, I have braces on my teeth. So
I will go when I take them off." I asked her if she is
going to be in Chiyoda during Golden Week (vaca-
tion). She said that she was going to "clean [her]
room" during that time. I said that I would be here
for a couple of days, and that maybe we could get
together then. I spoke to her in both English and
Japanese. As I was speaking to her in Japanese,
Keio said to me (in Japanese), "She speaks better
English than me, so please . . ." First he interrupts
my tennis game, and then he tells me what language to speak to her in. I felt he was being a bit
pushy. It also bothered me that he hadn't asked me
first—he just took the liberty of putting me on the
spot. She seems nice; I just hope I'm not taking on
more than I can handle.

My interpretation of Keio's behavior as "pushy"
suggests that I was viewing the situation from the (perhaps more American) perspective of an individual
rather than a group member. I felt put off by not being
given an opportunity to make my own decision about
whether or not I wanted to engage in a language
exchange with Satoko. This reflects an assumption that
we were operating from the premise that I was an individual and had the right to choose whether or not I

wanted to devote "my" time to this endeavor. I interpreted Keio's behavior as usurping my territory; however, as I look at the interaction from a distance, it
becomes clearer that he was operating from a different
cultural vantage point—from the perspective that, as a
fellow employee at the college, I was a group member,
without individual needs or rights. While at the time I
seemed to have felt imposed on, I can now consider that
Keio may have positioned me as an "insider" in relation
to Satoko, a newcomer to the college, which affected the
way he related and spoke to me.

In the following entry of our second encounter, we
see language learning taking place in the context of
other activities, such as talking on the telephone, riding
in a car, and shopping in a supermarket.

April 2

Satoko called me today. I sounded enthusias-
tic to hear from her. She seemed pleased that I
could recognize who she was immediately. I asked
her if she was free tomorrow. She said she was
going into Hiroshima. I thought for a moment and
said that I had some things to do in Hiroshima too.
She said that I could go with her, and, before I
could say whether or not I wanted to accept, she
was asking me when and where she should meet
me. I asked her what time she was coming back
and she said that she didn't know yet if she would
be coming back; she said she might go to her
hometown for the weekend. I thought again and
decided I didn't feel like spending $35 on the bus
and taxi (the bus stop is too far from campus to
walk) that it would cost to get back by public
transportation, so I said *ikemasen* [I can't go],
which I was afraid sounded a bit abrupt and possibly rude. Perhaps I should have ended with *ga* [but]
to soften it, but I didn't. She just said, *"Hai."* Then
she told me that she doesn't have clear water in her

room. She said it was *komarimasu* [troublesome].
This sounded as if she were asking me if she could
come over to use the water. My apartment was a
mess, and I was planning to do some work, so I
hesitated, and she said, "I guess I will continue to
gambattemasu" [work on it]. Then I told her she
could come over if she needed water to cook or
whatever. She said she had to go to Thanks (supermarket) first and asked if I needed anything. I said
I didn't have much here, meaning that if she
wanted to cook she needed to bring food. She said
she would be right over—and she was. My apartment was a mess. I hope it didn't shock her. She
stood in the *genkan* [doorway]. I told her to come
in, but she just stood there. I thought she was
going to go shopping and then come over, but it
turned out that she came over to take me to
Thanks. A complete misunderstanding. I decided I
might as well go shopping too. As we approached
her little, red sports car she apologized for her car
being "dirty" (it was spotless). We went to Thanks,
and as usual I went directly to the prepared foods
section. I picked out a packet of tuna sushi and
recommended it to Satoko. She bought the same
thing. She spoke to me only in Japanese. It
sounded like she was speaking naturally, and she
wasn't covering her mouth when she spoke anymore. I followed just about everything she said,
although I missed a few words. I noticed that I used
the expression *to omoimasu* [I think] a lot. Satoko
says *kana* and *kashira* ["I wonder" and "perhaps"]
at the end of almost everything she says.

On the ride back I asked her how she likes the
college so far, and she said how difficult it is being
a woman her age (30-something) studying at a college like this, where all the students are younger
than her, and that to suddenly change careers at
her age was a difficult thing to do in Japan, when

most people (especially her parents) tell her she should be settling down and getting married instead. I responded empathically. She also told me that she had graduated from a Japanese university and had been working as the assistant to the director of a hospital for the past 10 years. She said that her mother had told her to "stop this nonsense" about going to the United States, and when she had seen that Satoko was serious she had told her that she wasn't going to support her financially. Satoko said that she had lived at home in order to save enough money to study in the United States.

When we arrived back at my apartment I wondered if I should invite her in to eat the sushi, but I decided not to since my apartment was so messy. We talked a little about when we could study together. She seemed to take a passive role in this planning process, which made me wonder if she was still interested. I just left it open, saying, "Well, let's keep in touch." Then I thanked her (it seemed ironic that what was originally planned as a favor to her turned into a favor to me). I felt a bit of a weight—not very heavy, but a weight nevertheless—of being in debt. As I was leaving her car, she said, *"Mata aimashyoo"* [See you again], which relieved me of the fear that I had somehow offended her. It sounded better than *sayonara.*

This entry reveals that I was becoming increasingly more secure in my ability to understand meaning conveyed through hesitations, tone, and indirection. We see this especially when I was talking on the telephone, which was more difficult than speaking to someone in person since I could not rely on visual cues.

Satoko's way of speaking—tentative, modest, *yasashii* [tender, considerate, thoughtful], and ambiguous—was characteristic of the gendered way women have been traditionally taught to speak in Japanese (Lebra, 1984). Even when women are sure, they often say "I think," which is likely to be misinterpreted by English speakers as a sign of uncertainty. On the contrary, many Japanese women switch into tentative, feminine codes in order to be listened to. This is especially true when speaking to Japanese men, who generally will not listen to women who sound "too strong." Thus, women learn to sound unsure of themselves in order to express their opinions, while still being perceived as "feminine" and allowing men to perceive themselves as "masculine." Despite the timid and somewhat fearful way Satoko seemed to present herself, particularly when we first met, she struck me as a very strong-willed women, who, I was certain, would continue to pursue the independence and autonomy she was seeking.

Telling me her plans to go to the United States allowed her to shift out of the emotionally and financially dependent image her parents seemed to have of her. It also gave her an opportunity to express herself to someone who would take her seriously and not reduce her ideas to "nonsense." Thus, talking to me, in both English and Japanese, seemed to be a way for Satoko to expand and redraw the boundary lines that others have taken the liberty to set for her.

Perhaps due to our age or common interests and pursuits, I felt I could identify with Satoko more than I had with Keio and Akemi. This comes out most prominently in the many conversations Satoko and I had about being single in a marriage-obsessed society. Although both Keio and Akemi were also single and quite possibly felt some pressures from the environment to marry, Satoko and I seemed to find ourselves in a more marginalized social space. Whereas single men in Japan are referred to in a more positive light, as *bacheraa* [bachelor], Japanese expressions for single women portray them as "old" and "unwanted": "old

Christmas cake" [*furui kurisumasu keiki*], "unsold mer-
chandise" [*urenokori*], and "spinster" [*orudo misu*]
(Cherry, 1987). It is evident through the many times the
subject of marriage came up in our conversations that
it was a source of tension and anxiety. In private conversations we were able to mirror a sense of affirmation
and support of one another's single status; however, as
will be shown in more detail below, the images we had
of ourselves could not be divorced from the social context.

The diary entry above also reveals how not only the
family, but also organizational structures such as *giri*
and *ninjoo* function to keep people in their places. A
person who does not understand the concepts *giri* [what
one is expected to do] and *ninjoo* [what one wants to do]
is likely to encounter difficulty functioning in Japanese
society, for people become a product of their social
obligations and relationships to others (Kondo, 1990).
The concept *on* in Japanese characterizes a one-sided
relationship of dependence, which occurs, for example,
when one receives a favor or gift that one cannot return
with equal value, causing the receiver to become sub-
ordinated to the giver.

Evidence in my diary strongly suggests that the
vast majority of cultural knowledge I learned was
inferred through "habitualized practices," or, everyday
acts of doing (Bachnik, 1994, p. 14). The increased level
of activity I engaged in with Satoko compared with my
other language-learning partners, seemed to greatly
promote my language proficiency. This can be seen in
my increased use of natural, everyday language and my
being able to interpret Satoko's indirect and implicit
communication. My diary entries reveal lower inci-
dences of incomprehension and frustration while
speaking with Satoko. This seems to be largely attrib-
utable to both the more equal structure of our relationship and the emphasis placed on communicating,
rather than language learning. In the diary entry below

we see how empathic, nonverbal communication was becoming so salient, it sometimes seemed as if we were mind reading.

April 22

Satoko came over last night at 6:00 and stayed till 9:00. We had an interesting discussion in English, about some of the cultural and linguistic differences between Japanese and Americans. We talked about how in Japanese people pay more attention to tone and silence, and that Americans place a lot of emphasis on words. I expressed my frustration about the Japanese never saying "no," and described how Keio always says he will do something *"chikai uchi ni"* [in the near future] to avoid saying that he won't do it. She said this expression almost always means "no," as does *kanarazu* [definitely].

When we spoke in Japanese I noticed that she was talking faster than she was when she spoke in English, and that I wasn't concentrating so much on what I didn't know, but on what I could understand. There were only one or two times when I felt completely lost and spaced out, at which points she asked me, *"Wakarimasu ka?"* [Do you understand?]. I am constantly impressed with people's ability to pick up on this when I don't say anything. It must be the confused look on my face. I also felt there was a more equal exchange this time of initiating topics and that we both seemed to talk for the same amount of time.

She had brought kiwis, and I was peeling and slicing them. She talks in a much higher pitch than I do. My voice actually sounds low compared to hers. We're talking about what she eats for lunch every day and how expensive the food is at Thanks. I am half-listening and half-concentrating on peeling the kiwis. I try to say that I always take the free samples at Thanks, but I don't know the word for free samples. Satoko tells me, *"Shishoku"* [free food]. She commented on my *kawa mukugiki* [skin peeler], saying that Japanese use *hocho* [knives] to peel things.

She started to say something and then laughed, and I asked her what was so funny. She just kept laughing and I kept asking, *"Nani?"* [What?] Finally she said, *"Samugari desu"* [a person who is sensitive to the cold]. I asked her if she was cold. She responded by repeating, *"Samugari desu."* She wouldn't say directly that she was cold; instead she announced that she was the type of person who got cold easily. So I closed the windows.

I asked her to go over some verbs with me on my verb list. She used the words in sentences, which sometimes led into stories such as the time she was in *The Sound of Music* and became "nervous" [*agarimasita*]. When trying to use the verb *akirameru* [to give up], she told me how she is thinking about giving up on *omiai* [the practice of arranged marriages] since she can't meet anyone she likes. She described an arranged-marriage meeting she had recently. She went with her mother and the man went with his mother. She described the seating arrangement—the two mothers sat opposite one another and so did the prospective couple. She said that the mothers did all the talking while she and the man just sat there, nervously. She said everyone gets dressed up very formally. She said if the couple like each other then they go off alone somewhere to talk. She said she hates these meetings, so I asked her why she goes. She said it was because her mother spends a lot of money on them—20,000 *yen* (approximately $200) for each *omiai*. *"Da kara . . . giri no koto desu ne"* [So . . . it's an obligation].

We discussed marriage for a while. She said that more and more Japanese women would rather stay single these days. She said that men are still perceived as "higher" than women, and that this is reflected in the ways men and women speak and how men treat women. She said she has a group of friends in her hometown, all in their 30s, and all still single. She said she felt "comfortable" being single since she has this group of friends. They tell each other that when they get old, they can live together, and she thinks that would be a good idea. I agreed. She said that none of them had gotten married yet because no one has met an *ii hito* [good person]. I asked her what would be her idea of a "good person." She listed a few characteristics, such as having the same values, helping her with the housework, and "not bad-looking." I asked her if she asks the men she meets if they would help her at home if they got married. She said she could usually tell whether they would or not by their character—she said she usually meets only "self-ish" men. I asked her what it is about them that makes her think they are selfish, and she said she can soon tell when she talks to someone whether or not the person is sensitive. I said that I thought most Japanese people were sensitive. She said there are many different kinds of Japanese. She also said something interesting about people being nice to you when you know them only for a short time. "Once they know you for a long time, they are not so kind anymore." She also said that there is a lot of discrimination in Japan against single women—that it is almost impossible to adopt a child, and that it is difficult to get jobs and even apartments. She said in her last job, the men got to do more interesting work than the women, whose job it was to clean the office, toilets, and serve the doctors tea.

Listening to Satoko's anecdotes, I got the sense that, although she had accomplished many things in her life, her achievements were not often acknowledged. Her desire to be recognized for her accomplishments came out in certain contexts. The things she indirectly told me about herself in the context of practicing verbs may have been a modest way for her to allow herself to be respected for things she was proud of, rather than to focus on what she perceived she "lacked."

I could deeply empathize with her based on what I have felt and known from my experiences growing up in a society that not only does not respect, but that pathologizes, single "childless" women and aggressively promotes the "family" as the ideal unit, despite the by now well-documented evidence that it is all too often a breeding ground for pathology, violence, and fear (Ehrenreich, 1994). Barbara Ehrenreich sums it up succinctly: "For a woman, home is, statistically speaking, the most dangerous place to be" (*Time*, 7/18/94, p. 62).

Satoko's apprehension about being single was clearly audible as she talked about the strong sense of obligation she felt to marry (and as the eldest and only daughter in her family, this pressure was undoubtedly severe). Yet the structure of a support group—single women in their 30s banding together—seemed to help give her and the other members a feeling of belonging in a society that relegates its single members into a relative position of marginality, constricting not only their space to live but also to grow old and to die.

Takie Lebra (1984) "failed to encounter even one woman who was proud of being single or ideologically committed to staying unmarried" (78); however, she reported changes in the projected views of marriage among younger women below "the marriageable age." As she found:

[M]ore female (76 percent) than male (57 percent) students refer to marriage as a life stage, but 21 percent of the girls who mention marriage deny a married life to themselves while only one of the male counterparts does so. Two of these girls opt for suicide, and the rest want to remain unmarried as a matter of principle with the apprehension or conviction that marriage will thwart their pursuit of a career or freedom. Moreover, more girls, even when they choose to marry, tend to see troubles in the marriage, and more boys project marital satisfaction. (pp. 78–79)

Lebra suggests that differences between the sexes may be due to the stronger pressure to marry that young women feel from their environment, a pressure that becomes much more explicit and urgent as women near "the marriageable age."

Single mothers in Japan are often hidden from public view due to the severe stigma attached to out-of-wedlock births. It is also still unusual for nonfamily members to live together in Japan; although single, Japanese women such as Satoko were living with roommates, which may be signs of a new road paved for people who would like to choose a lifestyle alternative to the traditional concept of "family."

Although our commonalities enabled us to speak to one another fairly openly, one subject that was never broached was sexual relations or sexuality. My experiences suggest that sex is not a topic women talk about much to other women in Japan, or at least to other, non-Japanese women. However, erotic scenes are not censored on Japanese television and pornographic magazines are not stigmatized nearly as much as they are in the United States, which reflects significant differences in the ways "openness" is perceived and interpreted in the two cultures.

Although we did not talk about sex, we could not seem to avoid talking about men and marriage. As we see in the entry below, even just being out on a Sunday

afternoon, standing apart from all the (seemingly) heterosexual couples around us made us feel the sting of
the stigma many single women feel when they are
referred to as *sabiishi* [lonely] and not *ichininmae* [com-
plete human beings]:

April 18

Yesterday I spent the day with Satoko. She
picked me up at 9:30 a.m. and we took a drive to
her hometown. The weather was beautiful, which
made the hour-and-a-half ride very pleasant.
Everything has become very green and there were
pink cherry blossoms all over. Satoko talked a lot
in the car, in Japanese, about architecture—the
differences between the traditional and modern
Japanese homes—as we passed them along the
way. She talked a lot about how they were built,
what kinds of materials are used, and so on. While
I hadn't noticed much variety before, she pointed
out all the differences in the color, wood, quality of
clay on the roofs, and other materials.

When we arrived in her hometown, we stopped
at her house first. It was a huge traditional-style
wooden home. There was a strong scent of fresh
pine from the new wooden floors. Everything was
immaculate. Her mother greeted us at the door and
welcomed me, *"Irrashai, dozo,"* and I said the usual
customary expressions, *"Ojamashimasu"* [Excuse
me for bothering you] and *"Hajimemashite"* [Nice to
meet you]. Her mother, an attractive woman in her
60s, a bit on the heavy side, with a very expressive
face, made a pot of tea and served it to us with
manju [Japanese cakes] in a Japanese *tatami*
room. I tried to talk to her, but felt that my Japanese was terrible, and in fact it was. I apologized for
not being able to speak better. I felt somewhat
uncomfortable. Her mother offered me more tea,
but I said that I was fine, in very polite Japanese,

and she smiled. I complimented them on their beautiful home, which was really quite lovely, thanked her mother, and said good-bye—*"Oja- mashimashita"* [literally, "I bothered you"]—before leaving. Her mother said, *"Mata kite kudasai"* [Please come again], and stood waving us off as we drove away.

We drove to the train station in Mihara and took the train to Onomichi, a small city that is known as "little Kyoto" because of its traditional small streets, old wooden houses, and temples. It was a lovely place. Tons of people were out, having picnics and celebrating the cherry blossoms, which seemed to be exploding in full bloom everywhere. Satoko took on the role of being in charge of every- thing. She hardly asked me to make any decisions about anything. For the most part I didn't mind, but there were times when I think I would've liked to be consulted, for example, on what I wanted to eat for lunch. We stopped at an overpriced coffee shop where the only things we could order besides dessert were ham-and-egg sandwiches. I didn't say anything about not eating meat. I just removed the ham from the sandwich. Afterward, I discovered that the coffee shop used to be the home of a famous writer and poet, Fumiko Kobayashi. They preserved the room upstairs where she had writ- ten, which we were able to enter and look around. After lunch we climbed up to the top of the hill where there was a castle and 1,000 cherry trees. Satoko pointed out that this was a place where a lot of couples go, and indeed there were couples— young women and men—all over the place. We stopped at a shrine where we could wish for things we wanted. Satoko said that we had to throw 5 *yen* in first, pray for something, and then clap twice. I didn't have a 5-*yen* coin so she threw in a 10-*yen* coin and said it was for the both of us. I asked her what she wished. She said she wished that we would both find "nice guys." *"Ii desu ne"* [That's nice], I said. Then we took pictures of each other under the cherry trees. Satoko joked that they could be our *omiai* pictures. We walked around a lot in Onomichi. I enjoyed looking in the traditional Japanese craft shops and bought some *washi* [Japanese rice paper]. We browsed through some clothes stores. Satoko noticed that the things I liked were the same as what she liked, and she remarked that we had the same taste.

As we drove through the affluent area, all the big Japanese homes looked the same to me; however, as Satoko pointed out, differences in the wealth and status of the people inside could clearly be determined by outside appearances. Such attention to exterior details has the effect of making people highly conscious of how they look and are perceived by others. This phenomenon is reflected in the way Satoko and I, as two women together in a highly heterosexual environment, seemed to internalize an overwhelming sense of incompleteness, as if we had been built with inferior materials. Despite the fact that we had been having an extremely pleasant afternoon and enjoying one another's company, we could not escape the feeling that in some very significant way we were lacking. What seemed to come out, when we were in an environment in which we felt "different" for not being with men, reflects the power of society's mirror in forming our self-images: out in the larger world we could see ourselves only in terms of the way we felt other people perceived us.

My decreased ability to speak in the presence of Satoko's mother conveys a consciousness of having to switch into a different register for the social setting. In being overly polite and formal, I seemed to have been overcompensating for the stereotype Japanese have of Americans as informal and rude. The following entry provides a further example of how the intersection of gender, class, and age shaped the ways I spoke, felt, and perceived myself in relation to other women.

June 13

I met Satoko yesterday at 12:30 at a Royal Host in Hiroshima. I had originally planned to meet her at a Sunday Sun (these restaurants are chains in Japan, similar to Howard Johnson's in the United States) that I knew, but she suggested making it Royal Host since there are too many Sunday Suns and she didn't know which one I meant. I agreed, although I suspected I'd have some trouble finding the Royal Host, and sure enough I did. It took me 2 hot, grueling hours to get there. I had to stop at least a dozen times for directions. Satoko was waiting in front of the restaurant, and she drove off as soon as I got there. I followed until she stopped at a place where I could park. Then she drove the rest of the way to the place we were planning to go to for lunch. When I got into Satoko's car I was still annoyed about my ordeal trying to find the Royal Host, but the only thing I said to her when she asked if I was okay, was *"Sukarimashita"* [I'm exhausted]. She laughed in response, but I felt she got the message. My mood soon changed as I relaxed in her comfortable, air-conditioned car and left the driving to her. By the time we arrived at the Japanese restaurant I was in a much better mood.

The restaurant, which Satoko had picked out, reeked of elegance. As soon as we entered, I felt self-conscious about my casual clothes and wind-blown hair, which must have been all over the place. I suddenly wished that I had been wearing a dress and had my hair pulled back neatly in a ponytail. Satoko was dressed, as usual, casually, but she seemed very sophisticated and carried herself confidently in the restaurant, while I felt awk-

ward and out of place. The restaurant was serving
a special *Kaiseki* lunch. *Kaiseki* is a Japanese meal
served in many courses of very small but exquis-
itely prepared dishes. This was my first *Kaiseki*
experience, and I was surprised to see how tiny
each of the courses were. I think one of them actually consisted of a bean and a few seeds. Sitting
right next to us was a table of Japanese middle-
aged women dressed in beautiful *kimono*, which
made me even more self-conscious about how
clumsy I must have seemed every time I lifted my
glass or tried to pick up some of these tiny items
with my chopsticks. Satoko said that people usually have "lively conversation" while eating this
kind of lunch. She did most of the talking, mostly
about her new roommate—an older South American woman, whom she described (in Japanese) as
"the same age as my mother." I said she didn't have
to worry about being the oldest student anymore. I
didn't have any trouble understanding anything
she said—but I did have a little trouble talking in
the beginning. Then at some point, which I can no
longer remember, I began to feel more comfortable
and became less aware of being "out of my ele-
ment."

Satoko spoke a lot and very animatedly. I
noticed that when it took too long for me to
respond to something she said, she didn't wait for
me to finish, which ended my struggle—and
attempt—to speak. Satoko insisted on paying for
lunch, which came to about $80 for the two of us,
which was expensive, even by Japanese standards.
I accepted, and later paid for dinner, which was
much more casual and a lot less expensive. After
lunch we walked around a department store in
Hiroshima, and then she brought me to a Seventh
Day Adventist church to meet some people she
knew who were going to Iwakuni (a nearby town

that I had not been to before) to an outdoor restaurant famous for *omusubi* [huge rice balls] and grilled chicken on sticks, which everyone ate (including me), despite our claims to be vegetarians. The restaurant was called *Sansoku* [Bandits]. The group consisted of four young men in their 20s, the pastor, who was an older man, and one other woman besides me and Satoko. They were a friendly group. Almost all had lived in the United States (mostly California)—as Second Day Adventist missionaries—and spoke English fluently.

When Satoko first introduced me, almost all of the Japanese people spoke to me in English, but after they heard me speak Japanese everyone spoke to me in Japanese. This helped boost my confidence. The restaurant was very casual; we sat outdoors on tatami mats and ate everything with our hands. Everyone seemed very laid back and easy to talk to. I was able to understand everything people said and I spoke quite freely. I noticed a couple of times that Satoko covered her mouth when she spoke to the older man. The same person I thought was so self-assured earlier in the day seemed to become transformed into a shy girl—she spoke in a high-pitched tone of voice and ended almost everything she said with *kedo* [but] and *kana* [I wonder]. On the ride back to Hiroshima, at about 10 p.m., I was so tired I slept part of the way. Satoko was still full of energy when we got back to Hiroshima and seemed concerned that I was so sleepy. She offered to lead me part of the way back, but I said I'd be okay, and asked her for directions to the expressway. Although I could still listen to and understand Japanese, by the very end of the evening, I could only speak in English.

The exhaustion I expressed both in the beginning of the entry and again at the end reflects the tremendous amount of energy, time, and effort necessary to operate in a foreign language and culture. Since living with an American roommate on an American college campus was as close to living in a foreign cultural setting as Satoko had come, I sometimes felt that she was not as empathic of my situation of living in a perpetual state of semiconfusion as I would have liked her to have been, which may have at least partially accounted for the annoyance I expressed in the beginning of the entry. In retrospect, I can see how, in a parallel way, I too could not fully appreciate her experience of living away from home for the first time and sharing a room with someone who differed from her not only linguistically and culturally but also generationally. Despite our commonalities, our different world experiences made it impossible ever really to reach into and stand in each other's place completely. No matter how much we truly thought we understood each other, the world was indeed a very different place for each of us.

The above interaction provides further evidence of my increasing ability to communicate feelings through subtle forms of communication. This was undoubtedly due to being in a relationship with someone who I felt was listening—not only to words but to laughter, tone, silence—the "metamessages" (Tannen, 1990) of communication. We also see that I was becoming more sensitized to the subtext of what was being communicated nonverbally, through tone and body language. As Harumi Yamada (1991) says about Japanese discourse, "What counts is not what you say, but the feeling that you convey" (p. 43).

While earlier diary entries show a greater focus on what I was able to say in Japanese, entries of the later period consistently show that I was more actively listening and interpreting not only what was said but what was not said—even the silence. This strongly suggests that, in my development of Japanese, I may have cultivated greater skills in listening than in speaking.

This may also be at least partially a reflection of a communication style ("extension")[1] that I also used a lot in English: silence. However, it is important to remember that the language of silence is different in English and in Japanese.

Silent communication in Japanese is reflected in the language through words such as *haragei* [literally: "belly art"; figuratively: "silent communication"] and a host of proverbs that present talk in a negative light:

> *Tori mo nakaneba utaremaji.*
> [If the bird had not sung, it would not have been shot.]

> *Bijen shin narazu.*
> [Beautiful speech lacks sincerity.]

> *Aho no hanashi gui.*
> [A fool eats (believes) whatever is said.] (Yamada, 1992, pp. 39–41)

In other words, "Silence is golden."

Tentative, unfinished, fragmented speech is often not esteemed in English. In English, depending on who's listening, interrupted speech may convey nervousness, passivity, inarticulateness, and perhaps even insecurity. However, these spaces in between talk might also be perceived as providing greater opportunities for collaboration. The gap may be an opening into which a person can move, in order to follow or go on with the conversation, reinforcing the practice of cooperative action between speakers.

In both Japanese and English, the meaning of silence depends on the dialogical interchange: the extent to which a person's speech or silence is listened to and valued is determined by relational politics, or the larger forces that overpower the voices of individuals or groups in society. Like other forms of communication, silence is constructed through a give and take between internal and external reality. In communication among people who perceive themselves as equals there is a stronger tradition of, and greater respect for, listening. A person's silence in such an exchange is more likely to be acknowledged than it would be in a hierarchical exchange in which one person speaks and everyone else "listens." As Dale Spender (1980) notes:

> If cooperation (which implies being a willing listener as well as a willing talker) rather than competition and domination were to be highly valued in discussion, if 'talk' were seen as an opportunity for understanding the views of others and not just for airing one's own, we would witness profound changes which would not just be confined to mixed-sex talk. Many hierarchical structures, which currently permit and promote the talk of the few and the enforced listening of many, would be undermined. (p. 128)

My experience in the expensive restaurant Satoko and I went to replicates the strong internal sense I had when I first went to Japan, of wanting to find my place among a group of women, even if it meant having to change the way I looked, acted, and spoke. Conversely, I became more resistant to speaking "like a woman," or, *kirei na nihongo* [pretty Japanese], when I sensed that, by doing so, I was submitting to patriarchal control.

When eating the *haute cuisine*, I felt encumbered by the awareness of having to adhere to a certain form—how to lift my glass, use my chopsticks, sip my tea. My feeling inadequate in these areas made me conclude I lacked the "femininity training" the other women around me had received, such as "*elegance* in handling things . . . smoothness in the motion of the body or hands and discouragement of awkward or jerky manners" (Lebra, 1984, p. 42). Satoko's comment about people usually having "lively conversation" when eating this type of meal suggests that certain contexts are more conducive to women talking than others. That there were no male customers in the restaurant leads one to consider that the presence of men plays a role in the amount women can speak in order to be perceived as "feminine." In contrast to my feeling more comfortable and less self-conscious in the second gathering, when more men were present, Satoko's adjustments in her speech and nonverbal behaviors made her seem to me more childlike and perhaps less secure about her femininity when she spoke to the elder man than in the environment of all women.

The inhibition that I experienced in certain contexts described above appeared to be linked to feeling judged by my ability to perform certain social graces and behave according to ideals of etiquette that are different from those I learned through my own cultural experiences. The tensions—when I became insecure about my appearances and mannerisms, when I couldn't speak, when I perceived my differences as "deficient"—created important moments of learning that can easily dissolve without actively and critically reflecting on them.

For many Japanese individuals, going to the United States is an opportunity to escape from strong pressures to conform in a society in which people's identities are so powerfully shaped by the perceptions others have of them. But the Japanese who are entering the United States in search of freedom from discrimination must be troubled on discovering that Americans are not as free and liberated as we are imagined to be.

I was once again reminded of this thought about 1 year after I returned to New York City. I was in Central Park at the Gay Pride celebration, commemorating the 25th anniversary of the Stonewall riots. Surrounded by a crowd of lesbians and gay men uninhibitedly expressing their love for one another, I felt a great sense of joy and freedom. As I exited the park in a crowd, I walked directly behind a tightly interlocked gay couple. After several blocks the crowd from the distant park was dispersed and we found ourselves back in the mainstream. As we were crossing Park Avenue, I witnessed a haunting image. As if they had been pulled apart by huge magnets, the couple in front of me released their grip and stepped away from one another. At first they held hands, until finally they let go completely. They continued the rest of the way to the subway walking side-by-side without any sign of physical contact.

8

Travel, Confinement, Cookies, and Gender Reproduction

The diary entries in this chapter make for a collage of the social relations I had with a number of individuals in the community. My ability to participate in many of the events described in this section was contingent on my having reached a conversational level in the language; however, I was still operating from a place of only partial knowledge. While I had acquired more tools with which to interpret the culture, I was undoubtedly still actively *mis*interpreting situations, since I was reading things from a different cultural perspective. The diary entries of this section, then, include an analysis of how my past experiences and cultural assumptions came into play when interpreting interactions.

In contrast to one-to-one language-learning contexts, in which my interlocutors generally accommodated me in their speech, in natural situations I had to work harder to keep up with other people's language. Even when I didn't understand what was being said, I was actively involved in interpreting implicit and nonverbal aspects of communication, and thus absorbing the language and culture.

March 27

Last night I was invited to another one of Evelyn's (the Assistant Dean's) dinner parties. She seems to have developed this into a fine art. She arranged this get-together so that she could introduce the Horikawas, a middle-aged couple living in the area, to some of the faculty members they haven't yet met—me, Stan (the music teacher), and June (the Korean counselor)—both of whom speak Japanese fluently. The Horikawas have been active in the host-family program with faculty members at our school. He works at the post office and she works for an insurance company. They have two children who are both in college—one in Tokyo and the other in Kyoto. Bill, an American Japanese literature teacher, and his Japanese wife, Noriko, were there too. Bill has been living in Japan with Noriko for about 10 years, and he also speaks Japanese fluently. The conversation was in Japanese the entire night, probably because the Horikawas don't speak English. When I spoke to other Americans, however, I spoke in English.

I arrived with Stan. When we were introduced, Mr. Horikawa looked only at Stan as he spoke. Stan introduced himself in a very polite, honorific form—*"Dozo yoroshiku oneigai itashimasu"* [How do you do?]. I introduced myself slightly less formally, but politely, *"Dozo yoroshiku oneigai shimasu."* The expression literally means, "Please treat me well."

Dinner was served Japanese-style. We all sat on *zabuton* [pillows] on the floor. Evelyn and Noriko did all the cooking. Everyone else had brought bottles or fruit. I had brought wine. Mr. Horikawa was sitting next to me during dinner and kept refilling my wineglass every single time I took a sip. Everytime he did it I said, *"Sumimasen"* [Thank you/Excuse me] and held up my glass as he poured. Apparently Bill, who was sitting across from me next to Noriko, wasn't being as well attended to, because at one point he called across the table to ask Evelyn if there was any more wine. Noriko giggled. I think she was embarrassed. I complimented her on the dishes she brought, which were quite delicious, and she offered to teach me how to cook them. Bill bragged about his wife's cooking; Noriko said that he likes to eat—and he looks it.

Mr. Horikawa gave me his *meishi* [business card], and I humbly thanked him, as one does on these occasions. I hadn't brought mine, so I couldn't give him one in return. Then he began repeatedly to invite me to his house to drink sake. The first time I made a bowing gesture and politely thanked him, but the more he invited me the less formal my response became, until finally I just said *"Hai"* in an unenthusiastic tone of voice, which can also be interpreted as "I hear you." He seemed to be making a show of inviting me to his house. I glanced at his wife, and the expression on her face did not look as inviting as his.

I tried to sit *seiza* [on my knees] for as long as I could, but when it got too painful I sat sideways. Noriko and Mrs. Horikawa sat on their knees the whole time. I couldn't see how Evelyn was sitting, but I doubt it was on her knees. All the men sat in cross-legged positions. When a policeman arrived everyone—even the men—got on their knees to show their respect to him. (He was called when Evelyn's oven began to catch on fire.)

I did not have a great time at this party. It felt awkward and uncomfortable to be at an intimate gathering with people I hardly knew, and the conversation seemed rather boring, although the food was good, and as usual, I did a lot more eating and drinking than speaking. At one point Mr. Horikawa asked me if I wanted a "homestay." I said that I thought it would be interesting to get to know a family in the area. Then he said I could have a homestay at his house(!). At this point, Mrs. Horikawa made a comment about my hair, saying

it was *kirei* [pretty] and asking if it was natural.
Then she said that I was *kawairashii* [cute and
small]. I felt myself turning red. Then she asked me
several questions about my parents, what they do,
and if they are planning to visit me in Japan. I
shifted the subject to her daughter—asking what
she is studying at school, how old she is. Mrs.
Horikawa said her daughter is studying Spanish
and that she will be going to live in Spain for a year.
She said that her daughter is 18, "close to your
age"(!). I responded by saying that I was probably
closer to her (Mrs. Horikawa's) age than her daughter's. Mrs. Horikawa is probably in her early 40s,
although she did seem a lot older than I. Then, not
long after this pleasant little exchange, I took the
opportunity to make my escape as Stan was getting
ready to leave. I said *"Moo soro soro"* [It's getting to
be about that time]. Mr. Horikawa once again
invited me to his house and I said, *"Tanoshimini
desu"* [I'm looking forward to it].

As we saw in the previous chapter with Satoko, this
interaction also shows how pragmatic language-usage
was becoming more prominant. I was learning how to
use more highly restricted codes to hear things that
weren't being said and to say things without saying
them. This new way of communicating was not explicitly taught but was learned through shared cultural
knowledge. In other words, there was a degree to which
it felt safe to assume that Mr. Horikawa did not believe
that I was in fact "looking forward to" going to his
house. Rather, it was mutually understood that we were
merely exchanging polite expressions that were not
meant to be taken literally.

Increased comfort and familiarity in the setting
seemed to have given me a greater sense of security and
ability to make sense of and deal with a variety of situations, including getting out of those that made me

uncomfortable. Even though my interpretations may not have been accurate, I seemed confident in my ability to construct stories about what was going on. My ability to hear and understand nuances contributed to my increased tolerance for ambiguity. Thus, even though something about Mr. Horikawa's intimacy did not feel right to me, I did not experience feelings of anxiety, frustration, or feeling trapped by my inability to understand, as I had often expressed with Keio. An understanding of the structure of the language gave me more room to negotiate and get out of uncomfortable situations, by accepting without really accepting, saying no without saying no, saying yes without meaning yes.

We see this in the way I handled myself in response to Mr. Horikawa's constant invitations, which I perceived as both flirtatious and intrusive: although I was reluctant to say "no" directly, I was able to put him off indirectly, and thus say "no" in Japanese. My reading of his wife's reaction and questions also shows the beginnings of an awareness of the dynamic of others' feelings and nuances. More so than in earlier interactions, my grasp of what was going on was not just based on verbal understanding. "Subtle" forms of communication—intonation, hesitations, silence, facial expressions, ambiguous stock expressions—became more salient.

My diary entry reveals that I was more focused on what made me feel self-conscious and uncomfortable than on the actual conversation—the most pressing being the real physical pain in my legs due to having to sit *seiza*. As in the United States and many other countries in the world, there is a gendered way of sitting in Japan. Whereas men sit on their knees only under very formal circumstances (such as in the presence of the police officer, a highly respected position in Japan), women tend to sit in the more formal *seiza* position in almost every context.

A common expression used by Japanese men to

refer to Japanese women's legs is *daikon hashi* [radish legs], connoting a "short and stubby" quality in contrast to the long, slim legs many Japanese people associate with Western women. In addition to dissatisfaction with the way their legs look, some women complain of knee ailments, and "crookedness" developing as they grow older. This strongly suggests that sitting on their knees for long periods of time may not only affect Japanese women's legs aesthetically; it also can cause permanent physical defects.

That I sat on my knees, rather than with my legs to the side or crossed, which would have been more comfortable, reveals that I sensed my position in this group structure. Further, some of the difficulty I encountered concentrating on the large-group discussion may have been at least partially a result of a loss of mental energy—which became focused on the pain in my legs.

Another obvious source of discomfort at this party was my encounter with the Horikawas. My re-creation of the event in the diary suggests that I felt objectified and manipulated in the interaction. Especially when speaking to Mr. Horikawa, I seemed highly conscious of my physical gestures and carefully controlled responses.

While, for the most part, my way of speaking reveals a willingness to blend in for the sake of maintaining *wa* [harmony], I seemed to want deliberately to strike a dissonant chord in my response to Mrs. Horikawa's remark about my age. Clearly there were differences in our perceptions of what is considered "old" and "young" for women. Emphasizing that I was closer to her age than to her daughter's was a way of breaking the assumption that I wanted to be perceived as younger or of denying her implication that I should not be the age I was, 32. I was also annoyed at the feeling that she was trying to diminish me because she perceived me as a threat, when it was in fact her husband who was creating the threatening situation.

Mayumi and Me

The following diary entry focuses on an interaction with Mayumi, a married town resident whom I had met on several occasions at college and community functions. Although she was very soft-spoken and small-framed, and appeared meek, Mayumi was among the most outgoing and courageous of the Japanese housewives I met in this community. The extent to which she went out of her way to meet and know American people, and to learn how to speak English, indeed made her stand apart from other Japanese women in the community. Although she talks in our conversation below about her husband "letting" her have freedom to travel and participate in many activities that interested her, I was under the impression that, given that her two sons were still in school, she had a lot of autonomy compared to other Japanese wives and mothers, many of whom seemed to me to be more traditional.

My role in exchanges like these, as it often was with Satoko, may have been one of providing women with opportunities to connect with the outside world, to pull their inside experiences out.

April 4

Yesterday I met Mayumi at Murasusume, a coffee shop in town. I was stressed out at the time because that morning I had discovered that my computer had a virus and I had to meet her before I was able to take care of it. When we first began to talk we were speaking in two different languages (she in English and me in Japanese), which was getting on my nerves, so I suggested that we speak in English only for about 30 minutes and then switch to Japanese. She agreed. I just wish for once I could take a break from being an English teacher.

She asked me to call her Mayumi, not Mayumi-*san*. She said it sounded strange for her to

be called *san* [respect title (Mrs.)] by a foreigner.
This was very interesting. She added that sometimes even her Japanese friends omit the *san*. I
said that she doesn't have to use *san* with me
either. I was able to relax with her. She is a nice,
easygoing person. She also has a good sense of
humor; it's very subtle, but she's quick to laugh.
We seem to share a strong interest and desire to
speak another language. She said she wishes she
had been born in America. I asked why, and she
said that she likes English better than Japanese. I
asked her what she liked better about it, and she
said she liked the sound better. I responded by saying that I preferred Japanese sounds.

We got into a discussion about why we like to
study foreign languages. She said it was because
she could get different ideas and learn another way
of thinking. She added that most Japanese are
conservative and think alike. She told me that
when she had moved from her hometown,
Kitakyushu, to this area she had had to adjust to a
different way of speaking and acting. She said that
the people in the country are more conservative
than they are in cities. An example she gave was
that people were more reluctant to get divorced in
the country. I said that I thought divorce was a better alternative than being miserable in a marriage.
She agreed and talked about one of her co-workers,
a woman in her 40s, whom she described as having chronic back problems because of her husband
kicking and beating her. Mayumi has suggested to
the woman that she leave him, but the woman
doesn't.

When we switched into Japanese she told me
a story about a woman in her company who got
picked on a lot at work and whose husband went
to her office to tell everyone to stop bothering her.
But when the office workers told him that they

were just trying to "correct" her bad work habits, he took their side and beat her when they got home. We discussed some of the reasons men are so violent toward their wives. Mayumi said that men get angry if the wife doesn't cook them nice dinners. I asked her if she thought it might be the mothers' fault for spoiling their sons. She said it was both parents' fault. She said when there are male and female children, the parents usually tell the boy that he doesn't have to clean up "because he is a boy," but to the girl, mothers say, "You are a girl. You have to clear the table," etc. She also talked about her travels to New Zealand and New York. She told me that her husband "lets" her have a lot of freedom to travel. (How generous of him!) But, she added, he doesn't help her at home. She said that she works full time and when she comes home she would love to just sit under the *kotatsu* [table with heating lamp underneath it] and watch TV (like her husband), but she has to do house-work and cook dinner when she comes home. I asked her if either one of her sons helps her, and she said that because she is the only woman in her family she has to do all of the housework, although she said her sons serve themselves at the table and sometimes help clear the dishes away. I said their wives will probably thank her for that. I asked if they would help more if they were daughters, and she said, "I sometimes think about that." We also talked about a story that recently appeared in the news about a female Sumo wrestler who was banned from competing in the national champi-onships. I asked her her opinion of this. She said that it seemed very strange to most Japanese women for a girl to practice Sumo wrestling.

As we were leaving the coffee shop she invited me over to her house. I was still anxious to get back to my computer and said that I had a lot of work to do, but I agreed to stop by for a little while since it was on the way back.

The *genkan* [entrance] area had a lot of artwork displayed. Mayumi proudly informed me that they were all made by her husband. I sat in her living room while she prepared coffee in her kitchen. Her house was furnished completely western-style. The only signs of Japanese were her husband's calligraphy. She made some coffee and brought out a tray of cookies. I complimented her on the calligraphy, and Mayumi instantly volunteered her husband to teach me. "Oh no," I quickly said (in Japanese), "it would be too much trouble to teach me, and unfortunately I don't have enough time to practice." Her elder son, who is 18, came in a couple of times for some cookies. The first time he announced to his mother that he was hungry. She told him to take some of the cookies that were on a large plate on the table, pointing out which were the most delicious. He did as he was told and left. Half an hour later he entered again. This time he sat with us for a few minutes while he ate some more cookies. I said, in Japanese, "They're good, aren't they?" He let out a little laugh. I said something to him in English, thinking his mother would like this, but he seemed to get flustered and left soon afterward. A little while later he came in again for some more cookies. He didn't talk to me; he just sat nearby reading a newspaper. Seems extremely shy. Mayumi and I talked for a while and before I knew it it was 4:00. I said I had to go and thanked her. As she saw me off she expressed concern that I wouldn't find my way back. I assured her that I would. She said she will call me about calligraphy.

One of the most apparent differences in the Japanese society I moved into this time, as opposed to my earlier visits to Japan, was the more widespread acceptance by people in the community of my speaking Japanese. Due to the opening of a large American university in a small town, more people in this area were accustomed to foreigners than in the places I had previously lived. It did not seem to come as a surprise to the town residents that I could speak Japanese, but many Japanese people I met, particularly women, were very interested in practicing their English conversation with me. Thus, while the reasons may have differed from those in the past, it was still often a struggle to find someone with whom I could speak Japanese. Hence, the frustration I expressed at the beginning of the entry at always having to play the role of English teacher.

Particularly in situations such as these, when I was talking to Japanese women who, like Mayumi, so very much wanted to practice their English, I faced the dilemma of feeling a certain sense of responsibility to provide people with opportunities to speak English and of not wanting to deny myself the chance to speak Japanese. I found that, when I spoke Japanese, women who wanted to speak English asserted themselves in English rather strongly. This often made me give up trying to speak to them in Japanese (this was especially true during my first and second visits to Japan). Since this time I had been making a more conscious effort to learn Japanese, I felt I had to assert myself in Japanese more than I had before. It felt uncomfortable, however, as though I was involved in a kind of power struggle over which language to speak. However, negotiating which languages we would speak for how long (as I proposed in the interaction above) seemed to be a fair way of giving both of us opportunities to practice our respective foreign languages.

Although Mayumi was about 6 years older than I, her request that I omit the respect title *san* when addressing her implied a desire for us to have an extremely informal, familiar relationship, like that of people in the same family. This is a highly uncommon way in Japanese of addressing people one does not know well, which made the request seem rather unusual. I nevertheless did not have any problem complying; in fact, her request may have even contributed to my being able to relax with her, despite the anxiety and edginess I reported in the beginning of the entry. Not saying *san* at the end of her name communicated a greater closeness and sense of equality. This seemed, however, to be hiding a reality: we were in fact neither close nor equal. Nevertheless, I generally felt that we were able to relate to one another in a way that allowed me to concentrate more on the content of our discussion rather than on the structure of our relationship.

Even though the forms in which we encounter it in our daily lives differed significantly, Mayumi and I both seemed to be clearly aware of having to live under conditions of gender inequality. Although Mayumi talked about wife-beating as something that she has not directly experienced, the examples she gave of incidents of it among the women she knew clearly revealed a concern, and, at some level, a consciousness that it could also happen to her—for attention to the absence of violence in a relationship reveals the sense of a threat. Focusing on the severely oppressive conditions of other women may even be a way to escape confronting one's own subordination. However, the fact of not being beaten does not and should not minimize the day-to-day humiliation of control and confinement a woman has to put up with in her marriage.

While I closely identified with Mayumi's desire to travel, and to search for other possible ways of expressing herself and understanding her culture, I also felt distanced by a difference which, on some subliminal level, triggered in me deep anger and resentfulness. Her work as wife and mother struck me as a serious problem: even though Mayumi knew that different treatment for boys and girls created problems for girls, she still seemed willing to perpetuate these problems. I began to see her not only as a woman, but a woman policing, sustaining, perhaps even creating, oppressive conditions for other women. There was something about the dynamic of Mayumi's 18-year-old son telling his mother that he was hungry, and her not only telling him to take some cookies but pointing out which cookies to take, that in some way touched in me a basic need. It is in part the lack I feel from not having been mothered, but that lack has been deepened by the betrayal and abandonment I have felt from women who care for men in ways that they do not care for women, not even their daughters, sisters, or close friends. To be sure, if Mayumi's son had been a daughter, by 18 he would have learned how to open the refrigerator and take something to eat when he is hungry.

In patriarchal societies caretaking becomes so inextricably bound to being a woman that it creates a great imbalance in the ways men and women expect to be cared for. Because we give, receive, and take care differently, care cannot be assumed to mean the same thing to women and men.

In the 1960s and 1970s the women's liberation movement in the United States helped to draw attention to the problem of women's unpaid labor; however, as Gilligan (1982) points out, caretaking is still a great expense for women who have been socialized to devote more time and energy to others than to their own careers and interests:

> Women's place in man's lifecycle has been that of nurturer, caretaker, helpmate, the weaver of those networks of relationships on which she in turn relies. But while women have thus taken care of men, men have, in their theories of psychological development, and in their economic arrangements, tended to assume or devalue that care. (p. 17)

Living in Japan, I saw many social conflicts also relevant to American women's lives played out in the Japanese media. One popular Japanese soap opera that I watched focused on a young married women's struggle to go through medical school while her mother-in-law nagged her to take better care of her husband. The young woman emerged as the heroine: with remarkable endurance, she could achieve a medical degree, while being a devoted wife and dutiful daughter.

Another arena in which I saw the contradictory nature of Japanese women's lives enacted was in the real-life drama of the taming of Masako Owada. Although her initial appeal was her modernity—she was hailed as being an independent, internationally educated, well traveled, single, 27-year-old career women—as the Prince's bride-to-be, she played her part as a publicly silent, demure, controlled princess from the Tokugawa era. Women in Japan had mixed reactions to Princess Masako. Many younger women looked to her as a role model, wanting to wear similar clothing and accessories, and study in the same universities she had attended; yet some older, more independent women, who felt she had represented an opening for them, expressed a sense of betrayal and disappointment that a woman they had admired had ultimately capitulated to a severely gender-stereotypical role, albeit a high-status one.

There are many reasons why women comply with the patriarchy. For one, the basic need women have to connect with other women, even those who are being oppressed, seems to offset the tremendous cost of subordination. Further, in many societies women ironically submit to a patriarchical system in order to be taken care of financially. For example, in Japan, the custom of socializing the firstborn son [*choonan*] to take over the household makes mothers—consciously or not—partial to their eldest son, since he must be raised in a way that instills a strong sense of obligation and responsibility toward his aging parents. It is the daughter-in-law, however, who assumes most of the actual caretaking duties.

The historical record of gender discrimination in Japan dates back at least several centuries. It was first formally enforced in the Tokugawa (Edo) era (1600–1912), when the slogan "Good wives, wise mothers" was institutionalized by the government. More recently, in 1990, a male Japanese government official publicly announced that Japan's low birthrate and labor shortage were due to the "problem" of too many women going to college, as opposed to marrying right after high school. These historical and current events show how the legacy of gender-inequality viciously spirals down from one generation to another, perpetuating women's emotional and economical deprivation.

The diary entry above illustrated how, in the coffee shop, Mayumi entertained the idea that being a wife and mother was not benign, that indeed these categories could be dangerous for women. In the entry below, at her home with her husband and son, her perspective changes as she enacts these roles. The "problem" that comes into greater focus seems to be that of being alone.

April 11

Last night I went to Mayumi's house. She and her husband picked me up at 8:00 and brought me there. As I got in the car I said, *"Shitsureishimasu"* [Excuse me], and her husband called out, *"Dozo"* [Please come in] from the front seat. Mayumi and I talked in the car about spring coming, and *hanami* [cherry-blossom viewing] celebrations. I told her about my experience trying, but failing, to find the vegetable market that morning. She listened carefully, and responded sympathetically to me in Japanese, emphasizing my difficulty finding my way. She asked me if that happens in New York too, and I said, "Not usually." When we arrived at their house, I entered, again saying, *"Shitsureshimasu."* Mayumi responded, *"Irrashai"* [Welcome]. I felt somewhat more awkward and uncomfortable than I had the last time, when her husband wasn't there. He was presented to me by Mayumi as a very important person, and I felt I had to use very polite and formal language with him. He was a *shuji sensei* [calligraphy teacher], which seemed to command a lot of respect.

The calligraphy materials—brushes, ink, paper, felt cloth—were already spread out on a low table. Mayumi, her husband, and I all sat *seiza* around the table, first watching him do basic strokes. He gave me the paper he wrote on and told me to copy them. Every once in a while he would sit behind me, with his legs straddled around me, take my hand in his, and lead me through the strokes with the brush in my hand. This made me feel uncomfortable, although Mayumi who was sitting nearby didn't seem bothered at all. She also tried to write. We practiced seriously for a while, but I was pretty hopeless, and too tired to try that hard. I enjoyed watching him. He wrote beautifully. He showed me some of the things he was working on in class. I complimented him on them, but he rejected my compliment, vigorously shaking his head from side to side, and saying, *"Iie, iie"* [No, no]. I became more interested in watching him than in doing it myself. I asked him what his favorite word was, and he wrote it for me: *"wa"* [peace and harmony]. I asked him if I could have it and if he would sign it, and he became very flustered and excited. He seemed just like a little boy. Mayumi was the proud mother. She told him to sign it with his *hanko* [stamp used to sign one's name]. She told me that he makes wood-block print *hankos* and that he could make one for me. I wasn't sure how to respond. I said, "No, it is too much trouble," and never really accepted, but I didn't have to—Mayumi was already choosing the characters for the sounds of my name, "ka" and "ren." She wrote out the characters and explained the meaning—something small, delicate, and pitiful (!), but in a "cute," [*kawaii*] way, like a flower. I was embarrassed and said that the name didn't suit me well. They giggled and said, *"Iie, iie, sono koto wa nai"* [No, no, not at all].

After clearing the *shuji* materials away, Mayumi made coffee and brought out some small cakes. Mayumi and I didn't touch the cakes. Her husband had about four or five pieces. For some reason I felt too reserved to take any. I don't know why. She asked me what I was going to do the next day (Sunday). I said that I might go to Haji dam. Mayumi asked whom I was going with. I said I was going to go by myself. She had a very surprised reaction, and said, "You can't go by yourself—if you are going by yourself, please call me." She said this several times. I said that I was planning to ride my bike there. She said it was very far and dangerous to ride my bike by myself—it would be better to drive. Then she got up and did a few things in the kitchen. She said she was preparing me a *bento* [boxed lunch] to take with me to Haji dam. She also gave me a fresh loaf of raisin bread for breakfast. I said that I had plenty of food at home, but she packed it all up and gave it to me.

Their elder son was sitting with us, very quiet, but a bit more sociable than the last time. I tried to speak to him a little in English, which seemed to make his mother happy. He didn't seem to be able to understand. Mayumi spoke English in front of him and showed me her English homework, which was writing a recipe—*gobo* [burdock] salad. Her husband said, in Japanese, "She will make some and bring it to you," to which Mayumi surprisingly responded, in English, "Me? Why don't you make it?" Mayumi told me that he had taken a cooking course "for husbands" at the community center. She said that he had learned how to make a boiled potato with soy sauce. I asked how many husbands took the class, and he said about eight. I said that their wives must be happy. Mayumi agreed. I think they noticed that I was getting tired, and Mayumi asked me if I wanted to go home. I said, *"Moo soro soro"* [It's getting to be that time]. . . . On the way home Mayumi again told me to be sure to call her if I go to Haji dam. I said, *"Hai,"* knowing very well that I wasn't going to, and that she knew that.

Contrary to the experiences I had with Mayumi in the coffee shop, where I was lost in the conversation and focused on her, in her home with her husband, I felt much more self-conscious: feelings of discomfort, awkwardness, embarrassment, and uncertainty dominated my experience. One of the factors that clearly contributed to this was the presence of her husband, which anchored Mayumi and me differently in relation to one another. Whereas he moved and acted spontaneously and unself-consciously, Mayumi and I deferred to him as *sensei,* [master (of calligraphy)], and sat, spoke, and acted in a more controlled, self-conscious way.

Mayumi's husband's close, personal instruction in calligraphy seemed reminiscent of the intrusiveness I experienced in my encounter with Mr. Horikawa. Whether it was consciously intended or not, these men were taking liberties with me that I felt they would not have taken had I been a man, or a Japanese woman. While, on the face of it, their gestures may have seemed friendly, to me those gestures felt fraught with unconscious assumptions that made them reach me in a negative way. Their close physical contact and attention made me very uncomfortable, not only for myself, but also for the wives who were witnessing what I perceived as inappropriate closeness from people whom I was meeting for the first time. Since their wives did not show any signs (or any that I could read) that something was not right, I did not know how they felt, although I strongly suspected (or quite possibly projected) that feelings of discomfort were there, but well-concealed.

While there were similarities in the ways I felt with these two men, there were also significant differences in the two experiences. In the context of the public environment where many non-Japanese people lived, Mr. Horikawa was acting in a more false, disingenuous way, from a space outside of the culture; in the private setting of his home, however, Mayumi's husband seemed to be acting more humanely, from a place inside the culture. Had I studied calligraphy in Japan before or been aware that such close physical contact was a way of teaching beginners how to perform basic strokes, I might have interpreted his contact differently—perhaps as more "natural," and less awkward. In this and many of the interactions described above we have seen that communicating has less to do with the actual words and actions than with how our different histories behind us shape the ways we interpret an interaction.

There were also traces of similarities in the ways I felt Mayumi and Mrs. Horikawa related to me in front of their husbands. However, again, there were differences in the degrees of discomfort I felt. Whereas I sensed hostility from Mrs. Horikawa, I felt Mayumi was acting in a caring way. When she gave me a name in Japanese that meant something small, cute, pitiful, and delicate, I was given something, but it was a gift I could not refuse. Out of the many different *kanji* with the sounds "Ka" and "ren," why did she choose characters with this meaning? The characters she chose for my name depicted something that truly seemed endearing to her. The name she gave me revealed not only how she saw me, but how she saw herself in relation to me. Perhaps this name gave her a way to deal with the dilemma of my identity—as a single, unmarried woman in her 30s living alone, far from her native language, culture, and "family." If I were "small," helpless, "pitiful," and unable to find my way, she could help and guide me. This gave her a chance to relate to me from a position of power and authority, but not necessarily in a negative sense. The *hanko* [stamp] symbolized to me our solidifying this relationship. It created an image of me in relation to her that was literally etched in stone, and which would remain imprinted in Mayumi's mind, no matter how long or in what capacity we knew one another. Naming me may have made it possible for Mayumi to relate to me as a woman. At the same time, it wrapped me up in a confining social identity and assigned me a permanent position from which to speak.

In many ways I experienced something similar with Keio. From the beginning what Keio represented to me—a conservative Japanese "businessman"—caused me to have preconceived notions about him before I even knew him, which in part blocked my ability to learn from him. I felt more connected to Keio, and better able to understand him toward the end of our 5-month language exchange, when I began to see his humanity. My sense of his vulnerability as a person was triggered when I also saw him as a potential victim of racial discrimination. Then empathy, compassion, and a sense of solidarity mingled with the image I had of him as a dominant, controlling male.

Shuna, Noriko and Me: The Politics of Women

The various relationships I had with people in Japan reveal some of the changes that were currently taking place in Japanese society. For example, the intermingling of a traditional wife of a Buddhist priest (Shuna); of a Japanese woman in her 30s who has lived and studied in the United States, married an American man, and does not have children (Noriko); and of a single American woman in her 30s living in Japan (me) may be viewed as a microcosm of the increasing diversity in Japanese society. However, as the uneven power relations in our interactions reveal, plurality does not mean equality. Status within the group seemed to be based primarily on age, since Shuna, being the eldest, clearly had the most control over both the topic of discussion and the amount of time spoken.

April 15

I saw Shuna at the college today. At first she seemed distant. The last time I had seen her I was very busy and had no time to talk to her, so I wondered if she was upset about that. I asked her how she was. She told me about how she spent the last 2 days at a neighbor's home, where someone had recently died, preparing 50 *bento* boxes. She didn't express any feeling toward it; she just reported it journalistically. She also mentioned matter-of-factly that her husband was in Kyoto. She asked me about my plans for Golden Week. I didn't want to tell her about my travel plans, so I said I didn't have any yet. She pointed to a map on the wall and traced the route by boat to Pusan from Shimoneseki. I said jokingly, "Let's go together." She said, "That would be my dream."

I saw Noriko later, and she told me that she and Shuna were going to go to an *onsen* [hot-spring bath] later and asked me if I wanted to join them. I hesitated, but she said, "Please come," which made me feel like I shouldn't refuse. I asked her when they were going and planned to meet them later. We rode in Noriko's car—Shuna in the backseat and me in the front (in Japan the backseat is for people of higher status). Shuna seemed upset. She was complaining to Noriko that her husband went to Kyoto again, took their son, and left her home alone to take care of the house and temple. I asked her why she didn't go with them. She looked at me in disbelief for asking such a stupid question and responded that she has to *rusuban* [be the caretaker].

We soaked in both the indoor and outdoor baths for about an hour. Shuna was the first one to get out, and Noriko and I emerged shortly afterward. The hot baths made me sleepy, and then after dinner and a beer I felt myself easily slipping out of the conversation, which was in fast, natural Japanese the whole time. Before coming back, we stopped at Shuna's house, which was also a Buddhist temple, where we had some coffee and cake. Shuna spent most of the time talking to Noriko in heavily accented Japanese, which was almost impossible for me to follow, but I could tell from the tone that she was complaining about something. Noriko sat *seiza* the whole time, listened to her intently, and kept nodding and agreeing, *"Ne,"* after everything she said. I sat on my knees until they began to fall asleep, and then I sat with them to the side. The phone rang a few times, and when Shuna left the room Noriko began to talk to me. She asked me if I knew that Robert, a staff member at the college, tries to "hit on" all the single women. I said yes. Then she mentioned that another single male teacher sometimes goes to a "love hotel" with a student. I responded by asking if it was a girl. Noriko looked at me incredulously and exclaimed, *"Mochiron. . . .":* Of course a girl! What do you think, he's going to go with a boy? You mean he's gay!" I shrugged and said, "Well, you never know." There was a look of horror in her eyes. At the same time I was taken aback by the fact that she had no idea that there were gay men on the faculty, when it seemed so obvious to me. Luckily Shuna came back before she asked me any more questions, and they continued their conversation for about another hour. I stopped even trying to follow what they were saying and felt like lying down and going to sleep, but I just sat there and waited for them to finish. In the car on the way back, Noriko talked about her stay in Oregon when she was a college student. She said she hadn't made many friends because Americans were cold to her. She said the Americans at the community college she had attended sometimes had ignored her. She said it had upset her a lot. I said that sometimes I felt ignored too. She looked shocked when I said this. One of the last things Noriko said to me, as we pulled into the parking lot, was that she felt that some of the American teachers treat the Japanese students "like shit."

Who stands where in the hierarchy becomes evident in the way Noriko deferred to Shuna in her disciplined seating posture, polite way of agreeing, and minimal speaking. Although Noriko and I were the same age, our interaction suggests that she stood next in line. This dynamic was evident to me not only in my awareness of how much and the ways in which I was speaking and being spoken to, but in my consciousness of gestures—my place in the car, the order in which we got out of the baths, how I sat and moved my legs.

In contrast to situations in which the hierarchy is made clear through different linguistic registers and levels of politeness, I recall hierarchical situations in the United States that seemed to be masked by an egalitarian language. For example, I recently did volunteer work at a New York branch of an international feminist organization. The organization does a lot of very important work for women and the environment around the

world. The people who work there try to put feminist
theories into practice in the ways they conduct their
everyday work relationships, and, although this practice seems to be done with the best intentions, it does
not always seem to have the best results. For instance,
despite the fact that there are some extraordinarily
powerful women who work there, people try to be non-
hierarchical. The ways people speak and act toward
each other are explicitly the opposite of hierarchical.
The structure of the organization, however, is severely
hierarchical. Thus, it seemed to me that the language
was concealing—or even furthering—a certain exploitation, or mode of domination.

In responding to Shuna's question about my travel
plans I lied, so as not to make her jealous of my freedom. And when I later asked her why she did not join
her husband in going to Kyoto, I obviously was not asking because I did not know the answer. My reaction may
have been at least in part due to subconscious hostility
or anger toward what she and the traditional role as
wife, mother, and *rusuban* [caretaker] represented to
me. Perhaps I wanted to ask her a hurtful question to
jolt her out of a self-image that seemed oppressive to
me.

Some of my responses to Noriko reflect a similar
subversive communication style. The two instances
recorded in the diary above of when I spoke indirectly
suggest that this was a way for me to express something that was bothering me, or to get in my digs, so to
speak. Although I only alluded to the existence of gay
men on our staff, mentioning it was at least partially
motivated by my wanting to disturb what I felt was
taken as the given: one, that I should be invisible, and
two, that everyone was heterosexual. The fact that
Noriko had not considered that some of her colleagues
might be gay reflected a pervasive way of seeing (or not
seeing) in Japanese society, which seemed ironic when
public, single-sexed nude bathing was one of the most

popular national pastimes. While this bothered me, I also used the topic of homosexuality as a surrogate to make my own presence felt at a time when I had been feeling "ignored." It was an indirect way of conveying a certain hurt I felt for having been invited to join them but then made to sit for a long time in an uncomfortable position while being excluded from the conversation. I may have also resented that I wasn't getting a certain attention or recognition I seemed to feel I deserved for not acting "like an American." In other words, here I was, the low woman in the hierarchy, this American woman not being appreciated for not wanting to be treated as an American woman. The irony of this is that I wanted to assimilate but didn't want to give up a certain privilege—the attention and status of being American. This reminds me of the poster I saw hanging in the town hall of a man holding a baby (in chapter 4). The special recognition I seemed to feel I had coming to me when I was with Shuna and Noriko in some way parallels that which a man gets for doing something that in women is taken for granted, as if he is making a great special effort by taking care of his own children. But, in any case, I may just not have wanted to have been ignored.

It also seemed ironic that Noriko was so outspoken about the case of Americans mistreating Japanese, for her situation as the wife of an American man probably made her more of a target of Japanese people's discrimination than American's. This kind of discrimination is conveyed through expressions such as: *Kanajo wa yoko moji da kara* . . . [She writes her name horizontally, so . . . (she's an outsider)]. Such expressions, used by Japanese people to describe Japanese who, in their opinion, do not behave "like a Japanese," or "like a Japanese woman," make it clear that Americans are not the only ones who treat Japanese, as Noriko sharply expressed it, "like shit."

Interestingly, out of all the situations I described,

this last one, in making me feel the loss of my privilege, seemed to place me most inside the culture. It also helps us see that the special treatment and attention Japanese people tend to lavish on Americans working in Japan does not necessarily mean that we are perceived as superior. On the contrary, although I was permitted some entrance into the culture, by being invited into people's homes (and baths), the fact that I was not Japanese, or able to speak the language well, contributed to my having been excluded from this conversation, as well as others. As the saying goes, *Kanajo wa yoko moji da kara* . . . [She writes her name horizontally, so . . . (she wouldn't understand "our" situation)].

9

Arrival

Let me go back again to the beginning. When I was 19 years old, I traveled around the world alone for the first time. I moved around freely, open and trusting of people. Ten years later, when I returned to some of the countries I had visited, I discovered that the world isn't so hospitable to women. While in India I was raped by two men who I thought were friends. The experience was nightmarish and overwhelming. I was shaken into an awareness of how severe the penalties are for women who overstep their boundaries, either by thinking they can move around the world freely, or by maybe just one morning deciding not to make coffee for their husbands.

It deeply angers and hurts me that my prior educational experiences have failed to prepare me for what I have encountered as a woman in the world. I have gone through most of my life with very little conscious awareness of how gender was affecting what and how I was learning. After first being immersed in Japanese language and culture for 2 years in 1987, I experienced changes in the ways I felt, acted, and perceived myself as a woman. Since there are many different levels of politeness in Japanese, where one stands in the hierarchy in relation to whom one is speaking is more explicitly encoded in Japanese than in English. I became more aware of the role of social identity in communication, and that I was generally expected to defer to men. My desire to be accepted and recognized as a speaker of Japanese overpowered any subconscious resistance I may have had to complying with what I perceived as submissive female behavior. I also remained under the illusion that I was an independent, autonomous American woman who would be liberated as soon as I returned to the United States. This made it possible for me to play my role, at least for the time being, by speaking *onna rashiku* [like a woman] in Japanese.

The extent to which I was acquiring a Japanese feminine persona along with the language did not occur to me until I saw myself for the first time on a videotape, which had been recorded at the end of my 2nd year in Japan. As I described in the first chapter, I hardly recognized myself as the person who was sitting on her knees, speaking in a high-pitched tone of voice, and covering my mouth while giggling. What had happened then was mostly unconscious. On returning to Japan in 1993, this time to teach English at an American University in Hiroshima, I sought to look at these processes more consciously.

When I returned to Japan, I saw Japanese women from yet a different perspective. This time my vantage point, not only as a white, English-speaking American but also as a *woman,* in between cultures, sharpened my insight into how everyday language behaviors create and sustain larger social inequities. Observing from an insider-outsider perspective, I paid close attention to how people's language change according to shifting power relationships in different contexts. My diary gave me a tool to look within myself, to try to understand more deeply how I had been socialized to be a woman in my white, American, Jewish, working-class subculture and how I was learning to speak "like a woman" in Japan.

Because our personal histories shape how we see the world, and because no two people experience the world exactly the same way, even when the same language is assumed to be spoken, understanding remains incomplete. No matter how empathic and connected we may feel to another person, we cannot reach in and stand exactly where someone else is standing, feel exactly what someone else is feeling, or know exactly what another person is thinking. The awareness that all understanding is partial permits us to grasp that even people who are ostensibly speaking the same languages can interpret the same thing in a radically different manner. As we have seen, what one person might assume to be informal may be formal to another; an environment that makes one person relaxed may make another uptight; what might seem intimate to one person another may experience as invasive. Even something as seemingly neutral as the room in which a conversation takes place is not, because the relation of the people to that same environment may be profoundly different.

Less obvious than the physical environments, but equally confining, were the structural constraints embodied within the Japanese language itself, with its intricate codes of politeness and formality. Encoded in the Japanese language is knowledge of one's place in the social stratification. This is because the language is structured in a way in which levels of formality and politeness are adjusted to match the social context. The changes I made in the ways I expressed myself, my body language, the volume and pitch of my speech and laughter, reveal that in learning the language, I was also learning, quite figuratively, how to fit into a new social structure. We are molded by the structures of language. These structures give shape to some forms of expression, but for others, they provide no entry point. Language grabs hold of us: the grip can be comforting and secure; it can also be tight and choking.

The feeling of being contained in a structure of language, with no way to express certain feelings, or ask for what I need, reminds me of ways I have been controlled as a woman in my culture. At first I did not think that I was raised in a culture that enforces codes of femininity as explicitly as Japan, a culture in which women have traditionally painted their teeth black to keep them from opening their mouths and hid their faces behind fans; and where even today young Japanese women in traditional wedding ceremonies wear *kimono*—layers of thick cloth wrapped tightly around their bodies—and cover their faces in heavy coats of white makeup. Shifting my attention to what I perceived as the internalized oppression of Japanese women to the condition of American women, I began to see the ways women in my culture are similarly taught to deny or alter their bodies, by aspiring to be slim, covering their faces with makeup, shaving their legs, straightening or perming their hair, undergoing cosmetic surgery. These self-alterations occur in societies in which women are pressured to wear veils of youthfulness, which cover the wisdom of age and experience. Societies in which women are encouraged to be childlike, and are demeaned and punished for being "immodest," or for calling attention to their true physical selfhood, instill in women a cultural ideology of shame. On first observing such patterns of feminine socialization in Japan, I remained unconscious of how I had also been affected by these "subtle" forms of conditioning. The language I was learning in Japan was in fact not as foreign as it seemed.

My relationships with the various individuals I encountered in my language-learning journey affected both how I learned Japanese and how I perceived my identity. In some situations I was more self-conscious, resistant, compliant, and quiet, while in others I was more relaxed and expressive. The specifics in my diary reveal that these changes were related to the degree to which I felt located "inside" or "outside" the culture, and to how much I had to adjust to different social contexts and expectations.

The mutuality I perceived in my relationships with Japanese women helped me communicate across vast cultural differences. Focusing on gender roles gave us a way to begin to form a connection, but there were times when this focus obscured important differences between Japanese women and me, which kept us from understanding each other more deeply. Similarly, the dominant view I had of Keio as a man who was trying to control and "oppress" me through his didactic method of language teaching kept me from making meaningful contact with him. It is likely that the reverse was also true.

Focusing on how the dynamics of my relationships were affecting how I learned Japanese gave me a way to begin to understand a process so immense and complicated as language acquisition. In every linguistic situation there is a complex interplay between gender and other social structures such as class, race, culture, age, sexuality, and nationality, and one's language constantly shifts according to shifting power relationships in different contexts. Viewing language acquisition from this sociocultural and political perspective gave me a way of seeing the various forces that are at play in individuals and in groups in society, and sharpened my understanding that gender, like other cultural categories, is not merely fundamentally biological or foundational but a dialogical or dialectical process of constructing an identity in relation to another person or culture. Gender theories that do not acknowledge that we are different selves in different contexts cause us to be less than aware of how we react to the paradoxes of our multiple and shifting identities. The fluidity between identity and language creates a dynamic in which a person at once takes in a culture and is taken in by a culture.

The eagerness with which Japanese women wanted to learn English suggested that learning a new language may have offered them a different way of understanding their own culture and experiences as women in their society. For Akemi, who perceived herself to speak "like a man" in Japanese, going to America and speaking English may have been a way for her to separate from feminine role models she found oppressive in Japanese culture. She represented a tendency of certain younger women who are looking to other cultures as a way to get out of stifling situations. Satoko went to an American college to study English in order to claim autonomy and make some radical changes in her life. Yet her conflict of both wanting and not wanting to get married revealed a fear of gaining the sense of freedom she was pursuing.

To be sure, contradictions were a common theme in the lives of the women I encountered. Mayumi, for example, talked about gender inequality in one situation, but in another she enacted it in her own family relationships. Noriko knew what it felt like to be marginalized, silenced, and excluded, but she seemed oblivious that she was doing these things to other people. And there was a distinct tendency for women who had been more controlled by men, such as Shuna and Mrs. Horikawa, to want to control and discipline other women.

Although I met a wide variety of Japanese women, it was only a small sample in a country undergoing major social, historical, and economic changes. The internal turmoil of a society undergoing these shifts was reflected in the changes in Japanese women's attitudes I observed since my previous visits to Japan. There seemed to be more questioning—of family structures, marriage, women's position in society, of having to sacrifice femininity for career, self for family. Many Japanese and American women alike continue to struggle with these issues.

Certainly an important part of language learning is understanding words and grammar, but way beyond this, learning a language involves acquiring a role and knowing how to act according to that social definition. It is knowing, sometimes tacitly, sometimes consciously, what others approve and disapprove of, how to sit, how to enter a room, how to read nuances, when to speak and when to be silent, how to accept a gift, how to ask for a favor, how to ward off unwanted invitations. Knowing this is also inhabiting, sometimes consciously, sometimes subconsciously, a location in a socially constructed hierarchy: man-woman, teacher-student, husband-wife, son-daughter, married woman–single woman, American-Japanese. In other words, language learning, be it primary or secondary, entails a process of fitting into one's place in society, or rather, one's imposed place.

While academic conventions can encourage us to be impersonal, it may be precisely this point that causes us to be less than aware of the full personal dimension of all the sociolinguistic cues that comprise a person's social role in learning. Although it may be disturbing to reveal certain things about ourselves, the sources from which to bring about some real change may indeed be located in the places where we often shy away from looking. For in noticing where our rationalizations, accommodations, pain, and anger lie, we may begin to locate forces that oppress and liberate us. We may begin to understand not only our own particular problems, but how these problems relate to larger social patterns. We may begin to understand not only how we, but how other people are affected by these oppressive social structures. Then we might begin to understand how another person may feel. One person's story. Another person's story. Yet another person's story. And the personal becomes the political.

This basic tenet of the early consciousness-raising groups offers us a powerful tool to understand both ourselves and our cultures. It can help us understand how the political is already embedded in the personal. Yet even here there can be a danger—and that is coming to the conclusion that your experience and feelings are everyone's experiences and feelings. This can be very humbling, as it's easy to delude oneself into thinking one knows a person or a culture or even oneself more than one actually does.

As a teacher, I am concerned that people who make curricular decisions often mystify and obscure what it is like to be a woman, black, poor, working class, gay or lesbian in this society. Teachers of English as a second language are often faced with their own cultural identities and languages as they work toward negotiating meaning in an international community of learners. If we also consider gender and sexuality as cultural categories, which I do, the definition of "multicultural" becomes expanded to include all classrooms.

While cultural categories can offer a way of understanding and even sharp insights into people and situations, it is crucial, especially for people who work in multicultural settings, to understand that these categories can also conceal important complexities, for just as one mystification is lifted, another one can take its place. "Even the most powerful and accurate categories can freeze one into a place of partial understanding" (Roth, 1993, p. 67). Dewey (1954), was among those who recognized the "social pathology" inherent in such forms of mystification, "which works powerfully against effective inquiry into social institutions and conditions" (p. 170). Acknowledging our multiplicity—that we are different selves in different contexts—and that there are many different standpoints from which people attempt to view the same reality, can bring us closer to our awareness of the power systems in which we are defined in a given context. These implicit understandings of self in relation to others play a dynamic role in the mutually reinforcing processes of language learning and identity construction.

In addition to the natural curiosity that existed between my language-exchange partners and me, one of the things that I found helpful while learning language outside of a classroom was being able to switch roles from teacher to learner. In a language classroom, one way teachers can loosen the rigid boundaries that often exist between "teacher" and "student" is through sharing stories or personal experiences. Offering information such as where we come from, who we are, and what we do allow others to learn from us. Listening to learners express themselves in the second or foreign language may also help someone detect where there is a resistance, perhaps to the identity or the consciousness that the structure of the language may be pulling them toward. For example, a Japanese learner of English who avoids a certain form in English, such as gendered personal pronouns, may reveal resistance to a fixed structure that is negotiable, relational, and often omitted in Japanese. Or a person from a culture that emphasizes group harmony and interdependent communication practices who appears inarticulate or silent in a classroom may in fact be resisting an individualistic, competitive, and/or defensive way of speaking. Developing awareness of what they are resisting in another language may help learners recognize that different but related structures or ways of speaking may inhibit them in their own languages too.

Since I know what it's like to have these kinds of anxieties, I have arrived at a new understanding of the importance of trying to understand a language learner's cultural resistance. Some questions I might explicitly ask myself include: Is the student resisting out of fear? Out of insecurity? Is there something in the language that threatens the student's identity? Is the student resisting capitulating to a set of beliefs different from her or his own, which are either implicitly or explicitly embedded in the words or structure of the language?

Raising such questions in a language classroom is a first step toward increasing self-, cultural, and critical language awareness. The challenge lies in learning how to look deeply within oneself, because there's the potential for a lot of threatening material to be dredged up. This is not something everyone wants or feels ready to do, and it clearly should not be compulsory for those who are not comfortable exploring these issues. But I, like others, believe that our education should provide ample opportunities to reflect on, understand, and work toward changing those conditions that silence and oppress us. As Gordon Pradl (1992) says:

> Public disclosure and discussion of these appre-hensions, sharing stories of past educational dis-appointments and abuses, ends up going a long way toward liberating a new spirit and self-esteem. . . . As we talk about ourselves as learners, we come to acknowledge that weakness and inti-macy have an important role to play in education. (p. 17)

The "snapshots" of difficult moments in my life that I have exposed helped me trace patterns of the past to the present and make sense of feelings that I could not understand. This tracing has made me feel less isolated and more connected to others in the world; I hope oth-ers have also benefited from the telling.

It's often hard to know when a creative piece of work is finished. In some sense, it never is. Although I still have further to go, for now I will call this the end. Or perhaps I will call it the beginning. *Nagai tabi deshita.*[1]

Notes

Chapter 5. Keio and Me

1. See Kondo (1990) for a detailed ethnographic analysis of the politics of company workers in Japan. In her essay, "*Uchi no Kaisha*: Company as Family?" (Bachnik and Quinn's volume, 1994), she also provides an interesting overview of the themes *uchi/soto* as they relate to power in the workplace.

Chapter 7. Satoko and Me

1. Yamada (1992, 155) uses the term "extension" to differentiate a particular kind of linguistic phenomenon from "transfer." The former describes the use of a native speaker's style, or conversational strategy, in the target language, and the latter describes the use of a linguistic code. Transfers are considered interferences in learning the foreign language, whereas extensions are not. For example, a negative transfer (a transfer that leads to interference of meaning) that commonly occurs among Japanese English-as-a-Second-Language students is the omission of articles, while an extension may be a greater degree of indirect and nonvocal communication.

Chapter 9. Arrival

1. If you'd like to know what this means, there's a whole new language out there to be learned.

Bibliography

Aronowitz, S., & DiFazio, W. (1994). *The jobless future: Sci-tech and the dogma of work.* Minneapolis: University of Minnesota Press.

Bachnik, J. M., & Quinn, C. J. (Eds.). (1994). *Situated meaning: Inside and outside in Japanese self, society, and language.* Princeton, NJ: Princeton University Press.

Bourdieu, P. (1977). The economics of linguistic exchanges. *Social Science Information 16*(6), 645–668.

Buruma, I. (1986). Us and others. Review of *War without mercy: Race and power in the Pacific War. New York Review of Books,* 23–25.

Cherry, K. (1987). *Womansword: What Japanese words say about women.* Tokyo: Kodansha International.

de Beauvoir, S. (1972). *The second sex.* Penguin.

Ehrenreich, B. (1994, July 18). *Whose* family values? *Time,* 62.

Fisher, B. (1991). Affirming social value: Women without children. In D. R. Maines (Ed.), *Social organization and social processes: Essays in honor of Anselm Strauss* (pp. 87–104). New York: Aldine de Gruyter.

Foucault, M. (1980). *Power/knowledge: Selected interviews and other writings.* C. Gordon (Ed.). New York: Pantheon.

Gal, S. (1991). Between speech and silence: the problematics of research on language and gender. In M. di Leonardo (Ed.), *Gender at the crossroads of knowledge: Feminist anthropology in the Postmodern Era* (pp. 175–203). Berkeley: University of California Press.

Gilligan, C. (1982). *In a different voice: Psychological theory and women's development.* Cambridge, MA: Harvard University Press.

Haarmann, H. (1989). *Symbolic values of foreign language use: From the Japanese case to a general sociolinguistic perspective.* Berlin & New York: Bouton de Gruyter.

Kondo, D. K. (1990). *Crafting selves.* University of Chicago Press.

Lakoff, R. (1975). *Language and woman's place.* New York: Harper and Row.

Lebra, T. S. (1984). *Japanese women: Constraint and fulfillment.* Honolulu: University of Hawaii Press.

Lorde, A. (1984). *Sister outsider.* Trumansberg, NY: Crossing Press.

Rosenberger, N. R. (1994). Indexing hierarchy through Japanese gender relations. In J. C. Bachnik & C. J. Quinn, Jr. (Eds.), *Situated meaning: Inside and outside in Japanese self, society, and language* (pp. 88-112). Princeton, NJ: Princeton University Press.

Pradl, G. (1992, October 14). Teacher transformation through residential summer programs. *Ubs Responsen for Skrivlarare.* 2:1, 16-17.

Roth, R. (1993). untitled. In R. Roth and A. Sacher (Eds.), *And Then.5.* New York: The Magic Circle Printing Company, pp. 67-68.

Snow, C., & Fergusen, C. (Eds.). (1977). *Talking to Children.* Cambridge: Cambridge University Press.

Spender, D. (1980). *Man made language.* London: Routledge and Kegan Paul.

Tannen, Deborah. (1990). *You just don't understand: Women and men in conversation.* London: Virago Press.

Wetzel, Patricia. (1994). A movable self: The linguistic indexing of *uchi* and *soto.* In J. M. Bachnik, & C. J. Quinn, Jr. (Eds.). *Situated meaning: Inside and outside in Japanese self, society, and language* (pp. 73–87). Princeton, NJ: Princeton University Press.

Yamada, H. (1992). *American and Japanese business discourse: A comparison of interactional styles.* New Jersey: Ablex Publishing Corporation.

Index

DATE DUE

GAYLORD			PRINTED IN U.S.A.